I0149810

I'M NOT REALLY BLIND,

I JUST CAN'T SEE

BY

RONALD JOSEPH RANSOM

For the protection of individuals and families involved in this story, certain names have been changed from the original.

"I'm Not Really Blind, I Just Can't See," by Ronald Joseph Ransom. ISBN: 978-1-63868-199-1 (softcover); 978-1-63868-200-4 (hardcover).

Published 2025 by Virtualbookworm.com Publishing Inc., P.O. Box 9949, College Station, TX 77842, US.

DEDICATION

Because an autobiography is never the story of one person, this is not simply the story of Joe Ransom. This is the story of people. People that care. It is the story of how love and friendship can change one man's life. It is to these people that this book is dedicated.

> To Pastor Bennett and Pastor Bulluck for pushing me out of the nest.

> To Dr. Dalan and David Smith for believing in me.

> To James Hernando and Randy Schussman for being there.

> To Dana Calef for understanding.

> To Joe Teeter for being a friend.

> To Michelle for being herself.

> To CLC for giving me a chance.

> To Evangel and Central Bible College students, faculty, and administration for standing behind me.

But most especially this book is lovingly dedicated to Rick Knoth for never giving up on me and to Ric Muck for his labor of love. As Dorothy said to the Scarecrow, "I think I'll miss you most of all."

TABLE OF CONTENTS

FOREWORD

At the time of this writing, I am 25 years old and have been blind for the last two years. But I have seen without my eyes in those two short years what most people never have the privilege of seeing with their eyes.

Not having grown up as a blind person I was not prepared for what happened to me. As a child I read of Louis Braille and Helen Keller, but that was the extent of my knowledge of the world of darkness.

Like most people, I grew up thinking that all blind people lived in a world of total darkness. This is not so. In fact, most blind people can see, even if it is only light. Some blind people, along with the ability to distinguish light, can see color. Still others can see a vague outline if it is in a bright light. I have been very fortunate for I not only see light and color, but, with the use of my imagination, the foggy shadows I see can take on shape. For example, if I was in my drama classroom and I heard someone with heavy footsteps walk in I would begin my process of elimination. The classroom would show me that it was a drama student. The heavy footsteps would tell me that it was a young man. And as he walked by my desk I might catch a glimpse of bright orange from his jacket or smell his musk cologne. In this way I learned to "see" my world.

This is not so much the story of how I learned to cope with my blindness, as it is the story of how I learned to dream. And to work toward fulfilling that dream. For only a dreamer can truly see. - Ronald Joseph Ransom

ONE

The snow was coming down harder now. I curled up even deeper on the sofa as I wrapped the patchwork quilt around me and sipped my hot chocolate. Ah, Heaven!

I was very content with my life. I was involved in a small church in the mountains of Montana. I had a good job working as a dietitian in the local hospital, and I had a cozy apartment. I had no right to ask for more in life, but I had one lifelong dream. College. And since I had become a Christian that dream had enlarged to Bible College. Still, it was only a dream. I reflected on it as I poured myself another steaming cup of hot chocolate and sat down to read Dickens' A Christmas Carol.

Dickens was interrupted by an impatient knock at the door. I was surprised to find Ron Engstrom, the pastor's son, home from Western Bible College for the Christmas break. I had met him the week before. As I tried to invite him in he waved my words aside with, "Come on over to my place.

Mom has something to tell you. It's important. Hurry!" I grabbed a jacket and was halfway out the door before I had a chance to ask him what n the world was going on. He only smiled and said, "You'll be surprised."

The snow was deep and the walk to the parsonage seemed to take forever. Even after arriving at the Engstroms' home, it was some time before I could get any answers to my increasing questions. Mrs. Engstrom wanted to be assured, first, that I was warm and dry. When she could see that my patience had long ago run out she sat down and began.

"Joe, you've been dreaming about going to Bible College for some time now."

"I never said anything about..."

"You didn't have to. I could see it in your eyes every time you talked to Ron. You never talked about it because you were so certain it could never happen. Well, go home and pack your bags. You're leaving tomorrow morning for Western Bible College in North Dakota."

Silence.

"But there's no way! I have no money. I can't quit my job, and what about my apartment? I just moved in last week and..."

"That doesn't matter. I talked to your boss and you are free to leave. As for everything else, God will take care of you. I know that this is what God has for you, and if you don't go now, you never will."

"But if this is really God talking, He could talk to me about it. He could have told me about it before He told you."

"I think He did."

There was nothing more to say. If the idea was from God, He would have to talk to my landlord because no one else dared get anywhere near him. My hand trembled so badly I didn't think I could dial his number. One ring. Two rings. Three rings and no answer; maybe he wasn't at home.

"Hello,"

(Now, I've done it!)

"Uh, sir! This is, uh well, uh, my name is Joe Ransom and I'm…"

"I know who you are."

"Yes, well, I know that I just moved into your apartment and it's a real nice apartment and I like it a lot and…"

"Get to the point."

"Well, sir, I have to give you my notice. I mean, I have to move real soon. You see…"

"When are you leaving?"

"In about two hours."

"I see. You know this is out of the ordinary. I do require 30 days notice and an inspection of the apartment."

"I know but…"

"But in this case I'll make an exception. I'll not only pay you back your entire month's rent, but I won't even inspect the place. I trust you. Just stop by my office before you leave, and I'll give you back your money. Is there anything else?"

"Uh, no sir. Thank you, sir. That's very…"

"Good-bye."

This had to be from God! Two hours later I had packed what I could fit in a garbage bag and I was on my way to Allentown, North Dakota. Bible College, here I come!

Montana and North Dakota are known for their bad winters, and that winter was especially bad. I was used to snow-covered mountains and had often wondered if we would have such beauty in Heaven. But after we crossed the mountains in

Montana, I noticed that the closer we got to North Dakota the flatter the land became. And the flatter the land, the deeper the snow. The land was as vast as the ocean. Instead of billowing waves, I saw 10-foot snowdrifts. The snow blowing across the road reminded me of dust blowing across the prairie in an old western on TV. Then I noticed that the snow was no longer white. I asked Ron about it and he told me that it was from the pollution. I laughed at that because I knew better. We had been traveling for hours and had not even seen a car in at least three hours. I was beginning to think that there were more cows in North Dakota than there were people. Ron explained to me that the pollution was from the big cities— some of them as far away as Minnesota. Because North Dakota was so flat there was nothing to block the wind. The dust and dirt that blew in from Minnesota gave the snow an ugly color.

Suddenly the idea of moving to North Dakota no longer seemed so inviting. The land was flat and desolate. The snow was gray. The temperature was 40 degrees below zero.

Who did I think I was kidding, after all? I had no way to pay for a private college. If they wouldn't accept me, I had no money to go home. In fact, I had no home to go to. I was in real trouble. I could not afford to go to college, and after I got there I would not be able to afford to leave. Besides that, it was beginning to look like the North Dakota state tree must be a telephone pole.

Suddenly it loomed upon us. The most beautiful spot on earth, Western Bible College! At the end of Main Street you could see the girls' dormitory in all its beauty. The reflection of light from the windows shined on the snow. And the snow was as white as any snow I had seen on the mountains back home. In the center of campus was the new chapel with its cross reaching to the sky as a testimony to all who saw it. As I looked at this beautiful oasis all of my fears and doubts vanished. This was my new home. Surely this was where God wanted me. I remembered the sign I had seen as I entered campus: "Behold, He maketh all things new." I looked at my watch. It was just past midnight. Happy New Year.

TWO

Those first days went by so fast that it made me dizzy. I could not get over the idea that I was surrounded by 300 people my own age. And they were all Christians! My first stop was the chapel. It was to become my secret hideaway in the year to come. I climbed the stairs to the back of the balcony and found that if I curled up behind the sound room no one could see me. God and I were alone in our little corner. I could do nothing but cry out my thanks to a God who loved me so much! I, who years earlier had been a drug addict, was actually in Bible college. Never had a man been more grateful to God.

I knew that I had too much to do to stay in the chapel all day. It really didn't matter, though, because I could return any time I wanted to.

My next step was my real initiation into college life, the Line. The Line is famous on all college campuses. To register for classes, you first must go through the Line. And when hungry for supper, to eat in the cafeteria, first go through the Line. And when it's all over, to graduate, go through the Line.

My first Line was the registration line. I had been in line for over an hour when the student directly in front of me finally approached the financial aid director.

"Yes, I see that you are Linda Patrick. And how are you going to pay for your school bill?"

"I have a grant. That is, I think I have a grant, but it hasn't come in yet, so I'm not sure. But if the grant doesn't come in, I'm sure I can get a bank loan from home."

"I see. What you are saying is that you don't have any money."

"Yes, sir."

"I'm afraid you will have to go through that line in the next room and talk to my secretary. She will give you the proper forms to fill out. Fill them out and then get back into this line and I will see you. If it is after five o'clock when you get back into this line, then I will see you tomorrow. Thank you. Next."

"My name is Ronald Joseph Ransom. I don't think I'll be in your files. That is, this is, uh, this is my first semester here."

"I see. And how do you plan to pay your school bill?"

"Well, I don't know. I don't have a grant or anything, and I don't have any money, but I know that God sent me here, so He will pay the bill somehow, I promise."

"What was your name again?"

"Ransom, Ronald Joseph Ransom."

"Oh, yes, I know about you. You are clear to go through registration. Next."

I never did find out how they knew about me. I never asked.

The days passed on. I was given a room in the freshman dorm. I loved it. (Especially since it was next to the cafeteria.) I met my roommate and I started my classes. My new friends told me to be careful because the excitement of being in college would soon wear off. By mid-term I would find that these teachers I loved so much weren't afraid to give D's. And they promised me that I would soon tire of Wednesday night hamburgers in the cafeteria. They were wrong. Even after four years of college I could honestly say that the excitement only got better.

Not everything about those early days was great. I had been living on my own for several years before I started college, and I prided myself on my independence. I could handle things myself, thank you. It was very difficult to accept being in bed by ten-thirty. I didn't mind being told what to do during the weekdays but I felt that my social life was my concern and nobody else's. Still, I did learn to obey the orders I was given concerning bedtime (10:30 p.m.) And dating (only on weekends and no touching each other!) And study time (7:00 - 9:00 p.m.) And everything else the school told me to do. But my independence had a fight in another area. Because I had lived by myself for so long, it was very difficult for me to handle the idea of a roommate. In fact, I went through five roommates in four months. The first time I changed, I blamed it on my roommate. The second time, it was a coincidence. The third time, I admitted that I was a little hard to get along with. The fourth time, I realized that I had a problem.

I was sure that I was a real headache to many people that wanted to help me. The faculty was used to seeing students like myself and through much patience and even more prayer they eventually saw those students (or at least most of them) mature and graduate from college to become real men and women of God. The more I fought, the more they prayed.

One of the earliest answers to the faculty's prayers for me came in a way that I did not expect. Several of the students and I became close friends. These friends had more of an influence on my life than I realized at the time: Mark, Greg, Dawn, Virginia, Carol, Pam, and myself. Everything we did, we did together. These friends showed me how much we really needed each other.

During the day we saw each other in classes, in chapel, and during lunch. In the evenings we often went to the snack shop for a Coke and a game of foosball. Some of my most beautiful memories are of two or three of us getting together and praying for each other.

Our friendships had many interesting facets. Virginia and Carol were not just best friends, they were roommates. Now, that was fine except for the fact that I wanted to date both of them. Sometimes I think that the only thing they had in common was their differences. Virginia was loud and impulsive and rebellious. That is what made her so exciting. Carol was quiet and thoughtful and conforming. That is what made her so refreshing.

Carol saw me kiss Virginia goodnight once and refused to speak to me for two weeks. After two weeks of the brush-off, I knew that I had to explain to Carol that it was only a goodnight kiss. I put on my best after-shave and my only suit and set out to confront Carol. It was cold and snowy outside. I was especially cold because I did not have a winter coat over my suit. I bravely climbed the 13 steps to the porch of the girls' dorm and rang the bell. Eventually someone answered the door and I sent them with the message to get Carol. "And please hurry, it's cold out here." Carol must have known that it was me because she was in no hurry to come to the door.

She finally came out to the porch.

"Uh, Carol, I want to explain what you saw. It's not what you think." She stepped closer to me and I stepped back. "See, it was only a goodnight kiss." We each took another step. "Just ask Virginia, she'll tell you." As I took another step backwards I slipped on the top step and fell off the porch, landing in the snow. Carol was laughing so hard she couldn't stay angry. Besides, she said she had known about it all the time. Women!

Still, I didn't learn my lesson. It took me quite a while to figure out what was really going on. Carol and Virginia would cross- examine each other after one of them would go out with me. Then Carol would come to me and say;

"Joe, which of us do you like to be with the most?"

"You, of course."

"Do you have more fun with me than you do with Virginia?"

"Yes, I do."

"What do you like about me that's better than Virginia?"

"Well, you don't get angry quite as easily and you're a lot more feminine and..."

The trouble was that the next week I would have the same conversation with Virginia. When I was with Carol I did enjoy her more, but when I was with Virginia I enjoyed her more than Carol. They both saw this and all three of us knew from the beginning that nothing serious would ever come from our friendships so we never took each other too seriously.

If these friendships were my dessert, my studies were the main course. As I became more and more engrossed in my studies I became even more thankful that I was at Bible College. Within two months even I could see changes in my life. God was doing a major overhaul on my life and I was open for the changes God's work would bring. I was finally beginning to see that my problem was simply selfishness. I had spent my entire life living only to please me. And when a man lives only for himself, he can never be truly happy inside.

If a person is not used to opening himself up to others he will not be prepared for the pain that comes from loving. I had always felt that love cost too much. I wasn't willing to pay the price for love because I was afraid of being rejected.

THREE

Pam introduced me to Jami just a few weeks after school began. Jami was the kind of young lady that every guy on campus wanted to ask for a date, but none of them were brave enough to ask her out. Not only was she very beautiful, she was very talented. She sang, played the piano, and wrote gospel songs. She could even draw! She had long brown hair and her eyes smiled when she laughed.

I liked her immediately but I knew that we could never have a strong relationship. After all, she could have her pick of almost any guy on campus. She would be crazy to pick me. She was crazy. I never did understand why she wanted to spend time with me but I was pleased with her taste in men!

Dating at WBC was discouraged by the faculty and administration, so if we ever went any place together it had to be by "chance." We would often walk to the same bakery (there is only one in town) six or seven times a day. To this day, I still can't eat a cream-filled donut.

It was good to have someone to talk to, to share my thoughts with. We had common goals and dreams. We each wanted to reach a dying world for Jesus Christ. She wanted to be a gospel singer, and I wanted to be a Christian actor. Maybe we could work something out together? I began to enjoy the snow even more, because although Jami and I were forbidden to hold hands, I could put her arm in mine to help her walk on the icy streets.

Almost accidentally our relationship grew and developed. I had decided when I first came to WBC that I would not date until I had been there for at least a year. I wanted to spend my time studying and growing in the Lord. Jami changed that. I still spent plenty of time studying and trying to grow in the Lord, but now I did it with Jami.

WBC was a well disciplined school, but Jami and I felt that we needed even more discipline. Aside from classes and chapel we decided that during the school week we would not see each other during the day. And we would only see each other at night if both of us had completed our schoolwork. And even then, we would only see each other in a public place.

The discipline I forced upon myself, upon us, was good for me. It helped me mature much faster that I would have otherwise. The physical aspect of our relationship was never much of a problem. Both of us knew what could happen if we let things get out of hand, so we were very careful.

Jami was so pure and innocent that the idea of sex before marriage was demeaning. Just holding her hand was enough to please me.

As our relationship grew I knew that I was falling in love. This could never happen to me! I still saw myself as the short, freckle-faced, red-headed, cross-eyed kid that I was in the sixth grade. Although I was far from being a swan I was no longer an ugly duckling.

The Valentine's banquet was coming up and I wanted it to be very special for both of us. There are only two or three banquets a year at WBC, so the students take the opportunity to impress each other. I just had to impress Jami.

As I look back on it, I acted like a high school junior going to his first prom. I had never been on a "dress up" date before and I was inexperienced.

The first thing I did was to buy a new suit. Then I borrowed $10 from my roommate and went shopping. I went to every store in town. I wanted to buy the biggest, most romantic box of candy that I could find.

I am normally a very emotional, excitable person, and it is very difficult for me to act calm, cool, and collected. As I entered the banquet hall, Jami was already in line for dinner, so as calmly as possible I walked up to her and handed her the biggest box of candy either of us had ever seen. Then I took the corsage I had behind my back and started to pin it on her dress. She was beautiful and I was nervous. I was all thumbs and she started to blush. She wanted to help me but knew that it would embarrass me. Finally I turned to the man standing behind her in line and said, "Will you please pin this on her? I can't seem to work the pin." Now she was really blushing. It was then that I turned around again and saw what I had done. I had just asked the President of the college to pin the corsage on my date!

After Jami and I sat down to eat, it was difficult to start a conversation.

(Boy, Dad must be right. I don't belong in college. I belong on a horse in the backwoods of Montana.) The moment passed and we smiled at each other.

"I like your suit, Joe. Is it new?"

"Uh, ya'. I bought it this afternoon. It only cost $12 'cuz I got it on sale. It was in the little boy's department. I got a hat too."

(Boy, Joe, that was a dumb thing to say. Now she's really going to think you're backwards. Just cool it, will ya?)

"Uh, Jami, you're very pretty tonight. Would you like some more roast beef?"

Somehow I knew this wasn't working out, so as soon as I thought it was polite I said, "Jami, it's hot and stuffy in here. Would you like to take a walk?"

The fresh air felt good as we walked. The deep snow had been cleared from the sidewalks and it was nice to stroll around campus arm in arm. We sat on a bench in front of the chapel and looked at the light shining from the banquet in the cafeteria. For a brief moment I remembered the light from the girls' dorm that I saw my first night at WBC. No one would miss us at the banquet.

"Jami, I have something to ask you."

"Joe, I'm not ready for…"

"Oh, it's not that. It's nothing like that. Something's been on my mind and I need to talk to you about it."

"Is that why you were so uncomfortable in there?"

"That's part of it. Jami, why didn't you ever ask me about my eyes? You can tell by looking at me that something is wrong with them. At least one of them."

"Is that all that's bothering you? I mean, it's not like you're blind or anything. Besides, it's not important to me. You are who you are regardless of how your eyes look. It wouldn't make any

19

difference to me even if you were blind. I promise."

"Do you really mean that? Honestly?"

"Sure. Say, this is really bothering you. There's something you're not telling me. What is it?"

I stood and shuffled my feet. This was going to be harder than I thought. "Let's go inside somewhere that's warm. This breeze isn't good for us."

As we sat in the empty seats of the classroom I began again. "Jami, it is obvious that my left eye is blind. That is because of a freak accident at birth. My right eye was never very good but I could see pretty well with glasses. My parents always told me to wear my glasses but like most kids I never paid much attention to my parents. Because my eyesight was so bad I was never very good at sports. While my brother played football and baseball I was in my bedroom reading. It seemed like reading was the only thing I could do well. My parents always tried to keep me from reading too much because they knew that it was bad for my sight. I think they eventually saw how important books and schoolwork were to me so they were satisfied if I just wore my glasses when I read."

"I always knew, even as a little kid, that if I put too much strain on my eyes I could lose the only eye I had left. I guess I just never let it sink in.

Books were too important to me. They were the only true friends I had."

"Well, you know how college is. You can't help but spend most of your time reading. I don't want to alarm you or anything but I've been having some pretty strong headaches lately and I think I know why."

"But if it's your eyes, you've got to quit school."

"And lose my dream? No, I've got to get an education. Besides, I'm sure it's nothing serious. Probably just my imagination. I had to tell you because you're so important to me. I don't want to lose you. No matter what."

"Oh, Joe, you won't ever lose me. No matter what."

FOUR

As the next few months passed, Jami and I saw more and more of each other and our love grew. I began to think of my future as our future. I was in love. The only thing left to do was pop the question.

How to ask her to marry me was a real problem. I did not want to be like everyone else. I wanted it to be a special moment for her. I wanted it to be just perfect.

While Jami ate lunch I rehearsed my speech. I decided that right after lunch I would take her hand and we would walk to the park. We would sit on our favorite bench under the oak tree, and I would very romantically ask her to marry me. It did not happen quite as I planned. I walked into the cafeteria and saw her sitting next to Mark and Dawn. Mark knew immediately by my expression that something was up. "Hi, guys. Say, Jami, would you like to go for a walk with me?"

"Thanks, Joe, but I've got a lot of schoolwork to do. Was they're anything special you wanted to talk about?"

"Well, yes there is."

"You can tell me here. Cone on and sit down; I've got a few minutes."

"Well, I really need to see you alone. It's kinda' personal."

"I don't understand. What is it?"

I took a deep breath.

"Well, Jami, if I, not that I would, of course, but if I uh, well, would you? I mean you wouldn't have to quit school or anything, and I, uh, could get a job and work and uh, if anything happened like uh, you know, like what happens when people get, uh, you know, then you could get a job to pay the extra expenses and, uh, well you know what I mean?"

"Joe, I don't have the slightest idea of what you're talking about."

Mark and Dawn started humming the Wedding March and all eyes in the cafeteria were staring at Jami and me. This was not the way I planned it!

Not knowing what else to do, I grabbed Jami by the arm and ran through the cafeteria and into the snack shop below the girl's dorm. (Good! At least no one's down here. Now maybe I can propose the way I want to!)

I half pulled Jami to a far table at the end of the snack shop. She had figured out what I was trying to do, and she thought it was funny. She was really enjoying herself!

"Jami, I uh, well I really l-l-l-…"

"What was that?"

"Will you mar-r-r…"

"Are you trying to say something?" She tried as hard as possible not to laugh. She knew that I was trying to say 'I love you' and 'Will you marry me?' but couldn't get the words out. Just then Dawn came down the stairs and joined us at our table.

"I hope I'm not disturbing you." Snicker, snicker.

"You are!"

"Good. Proposals are such fun."

That was just what I needed! It was hard enough for me to deal with one girl, and now I had two of them to deal with. This was not my day.

I did not know it at the time, but while I was trying to propose to Jami, the snack shop was quietly filling up with everyone from the cafeteria. I would not have had a more attentive audience on the NBC Nightly News!

I could not stand it anymore. "Well, will you?"

"Not until you ask me properly." She had the nerve to smile!

I took a deep breath and leaned back so my chair was on its back legs. One . . . Two . . . three . . . "Jamiwillyoumarry . . ."

My chair fell over.

At that point the entire snack shop filled with laughter and applause. I had never been more embarrassed in my life. I grabbed Jami by the hand and pulled her from her chair. I pushed her between two Coke machines and squeezed in after her.

"Jami, I love you more than I have ever loved anyone in my life. I want to spend the rest of my life with you. Will you marry me?"

She did not speak. Her head was bowed and when she raised it and her eyes met mine I saw the wet spots on her cheeks. She was so beautiful! She nodded her head yes and smiled. For the first time I kissed her on the lips and we slowly walked out from between the Coke machines. As our audience saw us the room filled with cheers. Never had two people been more happy.

As the days passed I felt like a little boy again. My relationship with God grew as my relationship with Jami grew. For the first time in my life everything was going even better than I could have hoped for.

Jami and I were careful to spend most of our time doing schoolwork, and we were each involved in weekend traveling ministries. What little time we did spend together will always be a cherished memory. Snowball fights. Hot chocolate at the bakery. Walks around town in the cool evenings as summer neared. I had everything that any man could ever ask for.

Our first time apart from each other came shortly before the end of the school year. During spring break I decided to stay on campus and take a couple of classes while Jami went with a traveling ministry to several states in the area. I had two comprehensive courses during the break and I was thankful because it helped to ease the loneliness. I missed her so much. Her letters were filled with exciting news about the results of her work. I was just beginning to realize what a special young lady I was going to marry.

The headaches became more common during spring break, but I assumed that it was simply because of the extra schoolwork. After all, I had to write an entire term paper and I had only two weeks to do it. That would give anyone a headache! Still, I should see a doctor. I decided that I would wait until after school was out in May.

I was worried when Jami and her group did not return on schedule. No one had heard from the group for several days and by then the whole school was wondering what had happened to them. It was at breakfast a week and a half later that I learned that the team had just returned. I was determined to stay "cool" and not let her, or anyone else, know how much I missed her. Mark, sitting next to me, asked me if I was nervous.

"No, of course not."

"Uh, are you sure?"

"Of course. Why do you ask?"

"Because you just poured orange juice on your pancakes and maple syrup in you milk!"

Because I was not allowed to officially become engaged during my freshman year I was not allowed to give Jami an engagement ring. That really didn't matter much because I couldn't afford one anyway.

Instead of a ring I bought her a gold bracelet with her name inscribed on the front. On the back was the inscription: "Jami, I will love you forever, Joe." As far as we were concerned, that bracelet was more precious than any engagement ring would ever be.

The last days of school were filled with final tests, banquets, and tearful good-byes. It felt good to know that most of my friends would be back next year. (Honest, Joe, three months won't last forever.) Jami and I decided on a July wedding. As she went home to do whatever it is that young ladies do to prepare for a wedding, I made plans to buy a travel-trailer for us to live in. I had very little money and my new job at the restaurant held little prospect of a "Future" so we had to be very careful with our finances. I found a 20-foot-long travel-trailer that seemed perfect for us. It was small enough for us to travel in yet large enough for us to live in, at least temporarily. I enjoyed teasing Jami about it and told her that after we were married, the first time she chased me around the trailer with a rolling pin and I had no place to hide, we would have to move.

I moved to Stilltower, South Dakota, when the semester was over. I missed Jami but I knew that in one month we would be married. (Come on, Joe, you can last one month!) I planned on having a busy summer. I was involved in two churches in Stilltower and I was working in two restaurants.

Along with this I made the 80-mile round trip drive to Allentown whenever possible to see friends that had stayed at WBC for the summer.

Like others, I had believed that the true Christian never suffers real pain, that the Christian life is full of roses. I had forgotten that roses have thorns.

I was not prepared for the phone call in the middle of the night. No one ever is. The words on the other end of the line sounded hollow.

"Hello?"

"Joe? This is Mrs. Gilbert. Jami's mother."

(Why is she crying?) "Mrs. Gilbert, what's wrong? Is it Jami? Is she all right?"

"Joe, I don't know how to tell you this. There's been an accident."

"Wh-what happened?" I sat down.

"Jami is…Jami is dead,"

(No! It can't be. I just talked to her yesterday on the phone.)

"She had just picked up her…her wedding dress."

(Oh, no, Jesus, this can't be. Please don't let it be.)

"She was on her way home and this drunk driver, he…"

"Mrs. Gilbert, I'm so sorry. Is there anything I can do? I know how close you were. She told me so much about you. Please let me help. I've got to do something for you, for her."

"No. There's nothing any of us can do now. Joe, I know how much she loved you. She always tried to get us together before the wedding. I'm sorry it had to be this way instead of at the wedding."

"Mrs. Gilbert, remember, she is part of the bride of Christ and He called her to Him. That's the wedding that really matters. She is now with her eternal Husband, and she is happy beyond our comprehension. We don't understand how these things happen, but God knows and we must trust Him."

It was only by God's grace that I survived the next weeks. Somehow He gave me the strength to go to work. I walked as a robot. I was too hurt to cry. I thought that if I cried I would have to give her up forever. I still wanted to cling to her as long as possible.

After about two months I noticed that not every thought was of her. One day I realized that I had smiled. Another day I laughed. God's strength was sustaining me. I had never been more alone. And God had never been more real.

A few weeks before school was to start again I received a special letter in the mail. The return address was from Indiana. (But I don't know anyone from Indiana. Anyone except...) It was from Mrs. Gilbert. She had sent me the bracelet I had given Jami. Somehow it had been destroyed in the mail. It was broken into several pieces and I knew that it could not be repaired. I went into the trailer and knelt by the couch.

"Why God? It's the only thing I have left from her. Why did the post office have to break it? It's the only thing I have."

Quietly I was reminded of a picture Jami had drawn for me the night I gave her the bracelet. I dug through the boxes in the closet until I found it. I put it on the table and let my mind take me back to the night she drew it for me. It was a drawing of the empty tomb of Christ. Across the top were the words, "He is not here; He is risen". That was the way God wanted me to remember Jami. She was no longer here; she was in Heaven. At last I let the tears flow freely for the girl I loved. Good-bye, Jami. I will love you forever.

FIVE

I continued to work in the restaurants for the rest of the summer. While I worked in one of the churches in Stilltower I met a man who would become one of the best friends I would ever have. His name was Randy Schussman. We spent many hours sitting at his kitchen table eating his wife's good cooking and discussing the Bible. There were many things that we did not agree on, but we were both sincere and we were willing to change our minds if God showed us we were wrong. Randy helped to ease the pain of losing Jami. He took me in as his "little brother" and I am still his "little brother" today. God knew that I needed a good friend after Jami's death, so He sent me Randy. I will always be grateful for his friendship.

School started in September, but I did not feel ready to move back to Allentown. Instead, I stayed in Stilltower and commuted the 80 miles every day. It would have been too difficult for me to be surrounded by the active social life of a college campus. Pam, Dawn, Carol, Virginia, Greg, Mark, and I renewed our friendship and spent as much time as possible together. They helped me through the roughest time of my life.

When the first snow fell at the end of October I knew that I had to move back to Allentown because it was no longer possible to commute every day. I moved to a small trailer court just outside the city limits. With friendships renewed, at least three or four times a week we had pizza parties at my place. I enjoyed the company and they enjoyed having a chance to get off campus. Saturdays we spent doing schoolwork together. We all had a lot to learn about maturity but our love for each other really helped us.

My trailer had not been built with North Dakota winters in mind. The water heater was on the outside and every time the wind blew (which was most of the time) it would blow out the pilot light. The result was that most of the time I had no hot water. The trailer was not insulated and when the wind blew, a chill went right through. In fact, we could sit at one end of the trailer and watch the curtains at the other end move every time the wind blew. If it was a very strong wind it would cause the entire trailer to rock back and forth like a rowboat. That never stopped us though. We would cover up the windows and the door with blankets and then we would sit close together on the couch and put the rest of the blankets around us as we ate pizza and studied.

That was the worst winter I had ever seen. Because we seemed to be living in a perpetual blizzard, it was dangerous for me to walk to and from school by myself. It was impossible to get a vehicle, even a four-wheel drive, through the snow to my place. At one time the snow had so completely buried one side of my trailer that I was stranded at home for three days before I could get out. I had no phone, so I was unable to get help, and when the school noticed that I was missing, they sent a team of four men to try to find me. The wind was so strong that they had to walk arm in arm in order not to lose anyone.

As cold and as hard as that winter was, it was still very special to me. Winter will always be my favorite part of the year. The pain of losing Jami wasn't as strong anymore, and I was filling my time with making new memories. I was now able to remember Jami without all the hurt in my heart.

One of the most memorable times of my life occurred that winter. It was late in the afternoon and I was walking home from school. It was a clear and beautiful day but the wind was bitterly cold and forced me to walk with my head down to avoid the chill. I was within sight of the trailer court when I heard a large truck coming toward me. I looked up and thought that it was a strange time of year for a truck to be pulling a travel-trailer. The driver waved at me, and I waved back. I thought it was interesting that the trailer he was pulling was the same size and brand as mine.

By now I was at the entrance to the trailer court and I was stunned when I saw that my trailer was gone. I had just waved to the man that had stolen my home!

As I turned around I saw the taillights of my trailer fade into the sunset. I should have at least been furious. Maybe even frightened. But it was so ironic and so funny that all I could do was sit on the snow where my trailer had been and laugh! This was unbelievable!

The only thing for me to do was walk back to the school and report what had happened. They would never believe this!

It was several days before I discovered what had happened. In the meantime I stayed in the men's dorm with Mark and Greg. The faculty told me not to tell anyone what had happened, but when I went to class the next day wearing jeans I had a lot of explaining to do. Men were not allowed to wear jeans to class, but because the rest of my clothes were in the trailer I had no choice.

One of my instructors received a phone call a few days later and was told about my trailer. It seems that the water pipes on the trailer had frozen and it was causing problems for the other trailers in the area. Instead of notifying me of the problem the landlord simply took it upon himself to remove the trailer. It was sitting in his driveway, and would I please come to pick it up?

Because of that incident the school let me move into the men's dorm for the rest of the school year. My trailer would be safely stored behind the cafeteria.

Christmas came and went. With February came the Valentine's banquet. Again it was held in the cafeteria. This year I did not buy a new suit or a box of candy. I did not go for a nice walk around campus. Instead, I sat in my trailer. My memories and I. As I listened to the music from the cafeteria I realized that as much as I missed Jami, I could never wish her back with me. I would not do it even if I could. She was happier in Heaven than I could make her on earth.

Although much appeared to be the same as it was a year ago, some things had indeed changed. I had grown a year older. Jami was no longer by my side. My friendships with other students had grown stronger. And I was going blind.

I knew it for sure now, but I still did not admit it. My friends could tell what was happening, but we never spoke of it. They knew I would speak when I was ready.

It was harder for me to read for any length of time, and the headaches were becoming unbearable. I was scared, and when I finally went to see an eye specialist, he told me to quit school.

"And if I quit school, will I still lose my sight?"

"Probably. But it could be years before that happens. Your eye is infected and the more you read and strain your eye, the faster the infection works. Your optic nerve is damaged, and I don't think I can stop the infection. I can only postpone it, and that means you must quit school. At least for now."

"Doctor, if I quit school, even for a while, I know I will never go back. You said yourself that I will probably go blind even if I quit school. Then what would happen? I would be blind and I would have no education. That is not a choice. I am going back to school and somehow, someday, I will graduate. If I have to go blind, it's a small price to pay for an education."

As the school year came to an end I knew that I had to start making plans for the summer. Most of the seniors would be starting their new lives working in churches and other ministries. Most of the rest of us would be going home to our families when school was out. That option was not available to me. When I first left home, before I was even out of high school, I decided that I would never return to live with my family. It was not because I hated my family. It was simply because I felt that when I left home I was supposed to stand on my own two feet. Besides, my father and stepmother were living on a small government pension, and they did not need another mouth to feed. And I wasn't ready to tell them about my failing eyesight. Not yet. Why worry them?

I decided to stay in Allentown and work for the summer. I got a job working in a new restaurant in town and I loved my work. But where would I live? I did not want to move back into my travel-trailer. The memories would be too strong. Instead, I sold the trailer and bought a 45-foot-long mobile home and set it in the trailer court my other trailer had been in. It took quite a lot of pleading with the landlord to let me move back in, but since there was only one trailer court in town, he finally gave in and let me move my trailer onto his land.

As summer passed I looked forward to the coming school year with new expectancy. This would be my last year. At last I would graduate!

I enjoyed being with my old friends again. And now that I had a larger trailer we had more fun. We were constantly having surprise birthday parties. After about the fifth party I wonder how many friends were really surprised to be invited to my place when their birthdays came around.

At the beginning of the school year, I made a terrible mistake. One that I regretted for a long time to follow. A friend and I had been talking about what our lives were like before we came to college and I casually told him about my past.

"Joe, I heard that you used to be on drugs. Is that true?"

A flood of memories swept over me.

"Yes, John. But it was a long time ago."

"Tell me about it."

"Well, it started when I began high school. Things at home weren't going very well and I needed an escape. There was nowhere for me to go so I started taking pills and … other things. When I decided I couldn't stay at home anymore, I left. I moved around a lot but my problems always went with me. I started taking more and more drugs. It began to affect my schoolwork and that in turn made me takes more drugs. It was like a dead-end circle. Finally, on my eighteenth birthday I took too many pills, and when I woke up, I was in the hospital fighting for my life. That really scared me, and when I started to take a better look at my life I wasn't very proud of what I saw. I had ruined my health with drugs. I had been arrested for several minor offenses and I was on a fast track to nowhere."

"Then what happened?"

"I had pretty much lost all connections with family and friends, and I was struggling just to stay alive. And when I wasn't on drugs I was trying to support myself and work my way through high school. I decided that I needed to start my life over again, so as soon as I was released from the hospital I moved to a motel in Missoula, Montana, to try and get my life back together again. After a fight with school officials I was finally allowed to return to high school. Because of my past I was considered so dangerous that two schools would not accept me as a student, and it was only with a long, drawn out fight that a third school let me enroll."

"And you lived happily ever after, right?"

My voice cracked as I continued. "No, not exactly. By sheer will power I was able to stop taking drugs and by all outside appearances things seemed to be turning in my favor. I was able to get a job as a custodian and later I was able to work for the state forestry service. I moved into a two-room apartment and then as my finances increased, I was able to move into a small trailer house. In March, I even graduated early from high school."

"I don't get it. That sounds pretty good to me. What's wrong with that?"

I spoke slowly as I groped for words to express my feelings.

"Well, John, it wasn't enough that my physical circumstances changed. You see, I was still the same person inside. I was still restless. I had not changed. I felt dirty and lonely. I was no happier than I had been as a drug addict. As I thought about my life I remembered other people. There was a teacher in Tacoma, Washington. He was a Christian and a great influence on my life. He spent many long hours telling me about how Jesus Christ had died for me so that I could have a real, genuine life. And he proved his words by the way he lived. I had never met a man like that."

"And then when I was in the hospital for drug abuse, I met a preacher who came to the hospital every day to see someone from his church. This preacher really bothered me. He was always happy and friendly. Every time he asked me to visit his church I gave him a hard time--"Hey, man, I don't need that. I can make it on my own!"

"Finally I realized that I couldn't make it on my own, and several months after I was released from the hospital, I visited his church on Sunday morning. As the pastor shook my hand after the service, I told him that I would never come back. I came back that night. He spoke very simply that night and said that Jesus Christ died on a cross for me and that if I really wanted to live, all I had to do was ask Jesus into my heart and have Him forgive me of all my sins and mistakes."

"As millions of people had done before me, I knelt at a wooden bench and asked Jesus Christ into my life. And as Jesus forgave me for my past, I also forgave myself. That was the beginning of my life."

"And then you lived happily ever after, right?"

I laughed. "Not exactly, but it has been easier for me since then."

John thought that it was his duty to tell other people about my past. And as more people were told about the antics of my past the story grew, and the more it grew the less truth it held. Finally, the inevitable happened. I was called in to see the Dean.

I had been sitting in his outer office fidgeting for about 15 minutes before he called me in.

"Have a seat, Joe." He looked very serious as he eyed the papers on his desk. "Joe, it has come to my attention that you have been telling people some uncomfortable stories about yourself." He looked at his papers instead of looking at me. "That you have used drugs. That you have a prison record. The list goes on. What do you have to say for yourself?"

"Well, sir, as far as the list is concerned, I'm sure that there is probably some truth to at least most of it. After all, most rumors are based on truth. But no, it is not all true. That doesn't matter, though, because the things I am accused of doing happened before I ever came to WBC."

"As for your not knowing about them, frankly, sir, that's none of your business. I don't mean to be disrespectful, but whatever happened before I became a Christian should not be held against me. Jesus Christ forgave me a long time ago. And you don't ask all of the other students about their pasts, so you have no right to ask me about mine."

"Besides, if you look at your records you will find that I did tell you about my past. I didn't tell all the gross details, but my application for acceptance here tells you very plainly that I made a lot of mistakes in the past. And that's exactly what they are. Mistakes. And in the past."

"I see. Well, if I hear any more about this concerning you we will have to take action. What I am concerned with is the here and now, and if you do not bring any more attention to yourself, we will forget the matter. You may consider this as a warning. You are dismissed."

I was scared. From that day on I did not know how to act or what to say. I was afraid that anything I said could and would be used against me in a court of law. The stories did continue, and all I could do was pray for the man spreading them. I knew all along that it was John, but I couldn't hate him. I could only feel sorry for him. And pray for him.

That, as scary as it was, was not my major problem at the moment. I was seeing more and more doctors. And they all said the same thing. I was going to lose my sight. Schoolwork was becoming more difficult and I was finding it harder to walk to school, but I kept on. I had no choice.

During the first weeks of the school year I had met another man that would greatly influence my life. Jim Hernando. He taught Greek at WBC. When I could not take the pressure any longer, it was to him that I went. I told him the truth about my past. I told him the stories that were going around campus, and I told him the thing that I feared most. I told him I was going blind.

As the weeks continued, Jim and I spent a lot of time together. Whenever I needed a mature friend to talk to, I would stop by his office. No matter what he was doing or how busy he was, he dropped everything just to spend time with me. His friendship has always been very special.

One of my favorite things to do was (and still is) to cook for other people. So it was natural that Jim and I combine our favorite things to do. Every Saturday morning Jim would come over to my place and I would fix him a fancy breakfast. Omelets, toast, hash browns, sausage, juice. The works. And after breakfast we would sit and talk about the Bible and tell each other what Jesus was doing in our lives. It felt good to spend time with a friend and forget about my problems and frustrations, even if it was only for a short while.

I sensed for a long time that I would be called in to talk to the dean again, but I did not expect to have to confront the president of the college.

I knew before I walked into his office that I would be told to leave WBC. I was thankful that he let me talk to the committee in his office.

"Sir, I know what I am accused of. I also know that I am innocent. You have told me to leave, and I don't hold it against you. I can see things from your point of view and whether I am guilty or not isn't the issue here. It doesn't look good for the school to have me here, and if other people who support WBC knew about me they might stop sending you money. Or they might not let their kids come here. You are doing what seems right to you, so I can't argue with you. I just want you to know that somewhere I will finish my education, and no matter where I go, I will never say anything against this school to anyone. I love it more now than I did when I first came here. I am very grateful for all that you have done for me. As far as I am concerned, WBC is as close to Heaven as I will get on earth, and I will never forget this place. The best years of my life were spent here."

It was not until I saw Jim and told him what had happened that I let the tears flow. Why? Why did I have to be kicked out of school for something I did not do? And why did it seem like I would never graduate?

My first concern was to get back on my feet and start walking again. Yes, school had been interrupted. My whole life had been interrupted. But somehow, somewhere, I was determined to finish school. There was no question about it!

SIX

My mind reflected on the events of the past few days as I was jostled around in the crowded pickup cab. I had said good-bye to my friends and to their question "Where are you going?" I could only tell them that I did not know where I was going. I only knew that I had to leave Allentown, and I had to finish school. I talked the situation over with Jim, and he told me that I should go to Springfield, Missouri, because Evangel College is in Springfield; and since I wanted a drama degree along with a Bible degree I should at least check out Evangel. What could I lose?

A friend of mine was taking his family to Arkansas for the Christmas break, and he offered to pull my trailer with his pickup and drop me off in Springfield. So now I was in a pickup cab with him, his wife, their two children, and their pet dog. Needless to say, it was rather uncomfortable, especially by the second day of travel.

The roads in North and South Dakota were very icy at the time and my trailer was really too large to pull with his little pickup. Still, we decided it would be worth a try. In order to keep my mind off of the swaying trailer in back of me, I spent my time thinking about another Christmas break. Two years earlier at the same time of year I was moving to North Dakota. Now I was moving to Missouri. I had the same problem to face now as I had then. What if they don't accept me? My grades at WBC had been very good, so I knew that would not be a problem. But what would I do if WBC wrote on my records that I had been kicked out of school. If they did not let me go to school in Springfield, I would still be forced to stay there because I had no money and no job. I had been through this same problem before and God had helped me then; so surely He would help me now. With new peace of mind, I went to sleep with a shaggy dog on my lap.

The farther south we traveled, the more beautiful the landscape became. I had almost forgotten how beautiful hills and trees could be. By our second morning of travel we had left the snow far behind us. I was becoming impatient as we drew close to Missouri. I was going to make a new life for myself in Springfield, and God was going to work everything out for me.

It was about 11 o'clock at night when we finally reached Springfield. Our first stop was a service station so we could get directions to my new trailer court. The attendant had such a strong Ozark accent that it took us five minutes before we could understand his directions. Within two weeks I would not hear a difference between these people and the people from up north.

It was dark when we pulled into the trailer court, but the lights around the swimming pool exposed the colorful leaves on the trees. It was amazing to realize that two days earlier I was in snow up to my waist and now I was wearing a short sleeve shirt and enjoying 65-degree weather. As we pulled into the trailer lot and he turned off the ignition, we heard a strange clicking sound. The tongue on the trailer broke as he turned off the ignition. God had seen to it that the trailer went as far as it was intended to go, but when it had reached its destination, God let us know that it was to go no farther.

After I had been settled in for a few days and was becoming comfortable with the area, I decided to walk to Evangel to see my new school. Christmas had been a sad time for me, and I needed to lift my spirit. I was feeling lonely and more than a little sorry for myself.

It was a peaceful night for a walk. After walking for about two hours, I could see the campus ahead of me. Something was wrong. I enjoyed walking around campus, but for some reason it did not feel like home. Not like WBC had. Why, Lord? Then God spoke to my heart. He told me that this was not His place for me. At least not now. I would go to Evangel someday, but this was not the time.

As I walked toward home I thought about what God was telling me. And I wondered where God wanted me in the meantime. I knew that He wanted me in Springfield, and I knew He wanted me in college, or at least I thought He did. Could I have been wrong?

Somehow I took a wrong turn that night, and I did not notice it at first because I was deep in thought. Then out of the night came the school. Central Bible College. That wrong turn was not a mistake after all. As soon as I saw the school I knew that it was where God wanted me. CBC has a beautiful campus, and is even more beautiful at night under the campus lights. I stood on a little footbridge and listened to the water trickle as I prayed and thanked God for sending me to Springfield. I looked at my watch. It was just past midnight. Happy New Year.

I was very grateful that when WBC sent my school records to CBC they did not mention why I left school. God and WBC were very good to me. I was looking forward to starting school again. In the meantime I had two weeks to get to know my way around town. Because I lived five miles from campus I decided that the first thing for me to do was buy a bicycle. The bicycle made me realize just how much my sight was failing. I had 10 accidents in five days. My sight was so poor that it was no longer safe for me to ride a bike. That scared me, so I decided to see another eye specialist. The eye specialist put me in touch with a vocational rehabilitation center. My advisor at the rehabilitation center told me that I should quit school and learn a useful trade. I told him a trade was fine for a blind man but that I was going to finish college and asked if his organization would help pay my school bill. He said it would.

Up to that point I had received government grants which paid for most of my school. I worked in restaurants to pay the rest of my bills. But now I was finding that no one would hire me. No one had any use for a man that was going blind.

Because I could not find a job, I was having a hard time financially. Grants were still available to pay for most of my schooling, but it was hard for me to take care of my other bills. I had applied for a social security disability pension but it would be several months before I would receive my first check. I was trying to make my trailer payments, trailer lot payments, utility bills, and grocery bills with only $70 a month.

I had a stubborn pride and I refused to ask for help unless I had no choice in the matter. In fact my pride was so strong that as my sight continued to fail I refused to use a white cane. White canes were for "blind people." Instead, I used a walking cane and let everyone think I had a bad leg. It was easier for me to accept.

In late January when the first snow came, I knew I was in trouble. I had no money for heating fuel and I would wake up in the morning to find as much ice on the inside of my bedroom window as there was on the outside of the window. I went for long periods of time without food, and that was especially dangerous because I was walking 10 miles a day in the snow back and forth to school. The water pipes on the trailer all froze, and I went the winter without any water. To wash myself or my clothes I used snow that I brought in from outside. I was thankful for the snow because as long as I had snow I would have drinking water and water to wash with. I no longer minded the long walk to school because it was warmer outside the trailer than it was inside the trailer.

It was during this time that I learned about true Christian love. Several of the students at CBC found out about my situation. One of them bought me a warm winter coat and had someone else give it to me because he wanted to remain anonymous. Another student found an old oil drum and made me a wood burning stove for my living room. It smoked the place up quite a bit, but at least I was warm; so the smell of smoke was like the smell of a dozen fresh-cut roses. As he left my place he handed me an envelope. Inside was $60. I knew that it was a real sacrifice for him to give me that money, and I will never forget his gesture of love. Several other students insisted on buying lunch for me several times a week. God was meeting my needs in a very beautiful way.

I will never forget the first time that they bought me lunch in the CBC cafeteria. I don't think I had ever seen such a large selection of food in one place. At least that's the way it seemed. As I sat down with my friends to eat lunch, it was hard for me to hold back the tears as I thanked God for the food and for my friends. But as I listened to the people around me I could hardly believe what I was hearing. So many students were complaining about the food. It was cold. It was salty. It didn't taste like Mom's home cooking. Maybe it didn't taste like Mom's home cooking, but to me it tasted better than that. It tasted lake manna from Heaven. Soon after that, one of the teachers found out about my financial situation and told the cafeteria manager to give me lunch every day and to charge it to his personal account. That was true Christian love in action!

The highlight of the school year, at least as far as I was concerned, was my being part of a traveling ministry group for spring break. About 10 of us had joined together as a drama group, and we were going all the way to California to perform "Games Christians Play." Along with being part of the group, I would be doing some of my own Christian drama. Our team was to be combined with another ministry group, and there would be about 30 of us altogether. We were going to be traveling farther from Missouri than any other group from CBC had traveled in the past. I was certain that the administration office would be checking on us very closely.

For several weeks before we left, we met once a week with all of the other traveling ministries and we prayed together. We asked God to give us strength and to help us minister. And we asked Him to give us results. We truly wanted to be servants of God.

The more we rehearsed our drama, the more it became obvious that I was having difficulty seeing what we were doing. With a lot of help from other cast members I was able to look somewhat less conspicuous.

The two weeks spent in California changed my life in ways I would never have dreamed possible. It was a long, boring drive to California and our patience with each other grew short. We were traveling as a convoy, and it was hard for us to keep track of all the cars in our group—especially in a downpour. We almost did not arrive on time. Just about everything that can go wrong on a long trip went wrong. Flat tires. Burned up engines. The works. As we pulled into Texas in the middle of a snowstorm, one of the cars crawled its last mile and died. After a long delay and a reshuffling of passengers, we were on our way again. We pulled into Los Angeles about an hour before the church service was to start.

The church building and the people of the church were very special. The church was obviously built by a Spanish congregation. It was whitewashed and had a flat roof. The buildings of the church formed a square, and in the center of the square was a beautiful garden with large shade trees and little wooden benches. The church was beautiful, but at the same time it was very simple. The congregation was half Spanish-speaking and half English-speaking. Two services were always going on at the same time.

Our mornings were filled with drama rehearsals and painting the church. The rest of the day we would divide ourselves into two groups. One group would stay at the church and paint while the other group would go out by twos and walk the streets to tell everyone about the church and to tell as many people as possible about the love and saving grace of Jesus Christ.

Our evenings were spent with our "host" families. We had been divided into several groups, and each of us was to stay with a family from the church. The family I stayed with was Spanish, but they spoke English fluently. They were very good to us. I have never in my life eaten as well as I did during those two weeks. Our host mother spoke English, but, boy, could she cook Spanish! Our host family took us to see the sights of Hollywood. It was an unforgettable experience. One of the CBC students that stayed with the same family I did was later to become one of my best friends. His name was Dana Calef. After we returned to Springfield he would prove to be a valuable friend when I really needed one.

As much as I loved the drama work I was doing, the most important part of my ministry was being involved in the street witnessing teams that went out during the days. At first it was very difficult for me to start a conversation with a stranger and ask him if he knew Jesus Christ as his personal Savior. But the more I practiced and the more I studied witnessing from the Bible, the easier it became. We prayed that the people would be responsive to us, but we never expected God to answer our prayers in the way He did. At one home we were met at the door by two ladies that looked and acted like they belonged on The Waltons. They promptly told us that they had their own religion, and they had no time to waste with us. As we thanked them for their time and turned to leave, their poodle darted from its hiding place behind the couch and attacked us. He bit us both, but he did not do any real harm. His actions startled the ladies so much that they asked us back in; and as they bandaged our legs, we had another chance to tell them of the love of Jesus Christ. We talked to them for over an hour. Thank God for poodles!

One of the most obvious lessons I learned during my stay in California is what Jesus meant when He told His disciples how difficult it was for a rich man to enter the Kingdom of God. Most of the homes we visited were of very wealthy families. It seemed that the more money a family had the less they wanted to hear the Good News of Jesus Christ. They were content with their material possessions. It was sad to see these families trying to convince us that they had all they needed without Christ. The poorer people, however, received us gladly. They knew that something was missing in their lives and that what they were looking for was not money. By the end of my two-week stay, I knew that I would be changed when I returned to Springfield. I would no longer ignore my neighbors, but I would tell all who would listen to me of the love of Jesus Christ.

My strongest memory of the trip will always be of my last Sunday. That was when we were scheduled to perform "Games Christians play," and I was to do my other drama.

Suddenly, right before we were to go on stage I became so sick that I could hardly stand up. I did not know what was wrong, but there was no way I could perform. Then we heard our cue to start and I was pushed onto the stage. I had no choice but to perform! After I had said my first line, I began to feel at ease, and by the time I had said my third line I was no longer sick. I began to realize that my being sick was simply my body's reaction to my being nervous. It was a problem I would carry for several years.

After the play was over, I was anxious to find out the response from the audience. I had dreamed of a drama ministry for several years, and I wanted confirmation that drama could be used as a tool of ministry. The response was beautiful. Many people were touched by the message of the play and told me that God had used the play to change their lives. That was when God told me that my dream would soon become a reality. Yes, I would finish school and God would use me to minister through drama.

The long ride back to Springfield was filled with thoughts of what lay ahead. I was excited about what God was doing in my life. Yes, things would be different when I returned home. Home. I had never thought of Springfield as home before, but now the word "home" seemed to fit perfectly. I was going home, and for the first time in my life, I was homesick. It was a good feeling.

SEVEN

The day I returned to Springfield I received a telegram from my sister in Missoula, Montana. It said Grandma had died. By the time I received the telegram, the funeral was over. I was in California when she died, and no one could get in touch with me. I borrowed the plane fare from the school and immediately flew to Montana. It was too late for me to do anything to help, but it was important for me to make the trip. One thought was in my mind the entire time I was in Montana; I should have written Grandma one last letter to tell her I loved her. I should have telephoned her. Grandma had done more for me than any other person in my family, and I knew I would miss her greatly. I also knew that I would never again miss an opportunity to let friends know that I loved them.

While I was in Montana there was no way I could avoid letting my relatives see that I was losing my sight. But still I refused to use a white cane. I used my walking cane and did not discuss my eyesight. The subject never came up. There was nothing I could do in Montana, so I returned to Springfield after only a few days.

From the day I returned to school until the end of the semester I was noticing a change in my sight almost daily. By the time summer school was to start, I was no longer able to read print. Because I had become used to the idea of becoming blind and because I was so busy doing schoolwork, I did not have much time to feel sorry for myself. I did not feel the shock that I would have felt if I had lost my sight in a sudden accident. And the more I studied my Bible, the more I saw that even if I did not understand what was happening, God knew all about it, and that was what was important. If God had a reason for me to be blind, if He could use me more effectively if I was blind, then I would not complain. I knew that God had the power to heal me and that if He did I would be thankful; but if He chose not to heal me, I would not complain. Besides, I would be healed in Heaven anyway. Either way I could not lose.

My world changed completely. The thing that was the hardest for me to accept was that I could not read print. That was especially difficult for me because I had to do my schoolwork somehow. And that was how Michelle came into my life. Michelle was a very beautiful blind girl. She was attending Evangel College part-time, and she worked at the Springfield Association for the Blind. She had been blind since birth, and she was very adept at reading Braille. From the first time that she came to my home to give me Braille lessons, I was impressed with her. She had a beautiful personality, and I was told that she was just as beautiful on the outside as she was on the inside. She was very beautiful indeed.

I needed to learn Braille very quickly and forced myself to learn the Braille alphabet in two weeks. My fingers were not yet sensitive enough to read the small dots, but I was at least able to take notes in Braille. It was a small start, but it was still a start.

By then my walking cane was useless to me, and I had to do the one thing I never wanted to do. I had to learn to use a white cane. The first cane I was given was made of wood, and I was rather awkward with it until Michelle taught me how to use it properly. As much as I had accepted the idea of going blind there was still a part of me that was scared. I was afraid of what being blind would do to me as a person. I had to release my fears and hurts from inside. After Michelle had given me my first lesson on how to use a cane and had gone home, I went outside to practice. I tripped on the cane and that triggered a response from emotions deep inside me. I grabbed the cane by its handle and swung with all my might at the nearest tree. As I hit the tree I yelled, "It isn't fair! I don't want to be blind!" I cried as I heard the cane break in two.

After that outburst it was easier for me to accept the things to come. Dana Calef, the friend from my drama team, needed a place to stay for the summer. I invited him to stay at my place for as long as he liked. I don't think I could have managed those first few months alone. I had to learn to do everything all over again.

I could no longer do the things I had taken for granted for so many years. How does a blind man cook or do his grocery shopping or walk to school? I needed answers to my questions, but I decided to get my answers on my own. I still had too much pride to ask for help.

The first problem to overcome was transportation to and from school. Dana and I both had early morning classes, so I was able to ride to school with him. My highlight of the day was to ride to school on his motorcycle. I loved the cold air blowing over me. It woke me up and prepared me for my studies. He worked in the afternoon, so I was forced to walk home alone. I had walked to and from school when I could see, so I was familiar with the roads. I learned to listen much more closely to traffic. Many people think that when a person becomes blind his hearing improves. I'm not sure I believe that. I think the blind person just pays closer attention to the sounds around him. And the white cane that I had avoided for so long was now a close friend. I learned how to feel the difference between gravel and pavement with just a quick touch of the tip of the cane. My advisor at the Bureau for the Blind began to tease me because I wore out the tips of my cane so quickly. After all, I was walking farther in one day than most college students drove their cars in a week. I was walking 300 miles a months!

Cooking was another problem for me and poor Dana had to put up with a lot of it. Because Dana worked during the day and paid for most of the food, I felt that I should do most of the cooking. I was thankful that Grandma had been the one to teach me how to cook. I don't think that Grandma had ever owned a cookbook. When I was younger and I would ask her for a recipe, she would laugh and say, "Joe, there is no recipe for that." And she was probably right. Grandma was German, and there was no American equivalent for most of her cooking. I had started grade school before I found out that you could buy a loaf of bread at the corner grocery store.

Grandma had taught me how to bake pies and check bread dough by the feel of the dough in my hands. So that was how I did all of my cooking. By feel. I was still very poor at reading Braille, but I did occasionally check my Braille cookbooks. When your hands are in the middle of your bread dough and you have forgotten what to do next, you have to take your hands out of the dough and wash and dry them before you can check your recipe. And if you have to do it very often you lose a lot of precious time.

Another problem with my cooking was the kinds of foods that I cooked. My parents raised me with the philosophy that a man is made of meat and potatoes. That was about all I knew how to fix. Dana, however, was a health nut and could live on fresh fruit and vegetables. I had never cooked with fresh fruit and vegetables and had no idea what I was doing when I cooked with them. Dana agreed with me.

Dana and I found another difference in our taste for food. I had always had a very limited income so I usually bought the cheapest things I could find. I pinched my pennies at least twice before I spent them. Dana paid no attention to price tags, and many evenings we sounded like a married couple as we argued about finances. After one such argument, Dana decided to be nice to me and do the grocery shopping himself. When it came time for him to buy the vegetables, he knew that I would be happy if he bought the cheapest vegetables he could find, so he bought several cans of vegetables on sale. I laughed as I told him that a blind person can not tell the difference between a can of corn and a can of peas. From then on he bought frozen bags of vegetables, and I never complained about the way he bought groceries.

It wasn't as hard as I thought it would be for me to go grocery shopping my myself. There was a small fast food store two blocks from home, and that is where I was to make my first trial run. Most single people do not buy a large variety of food, so they generally do their shopping the same way every week. It was simply a matter of memorization for me. I could smell the bread, so it was easy to find at least that product. By checking the size of the loaf I knew if it was the sandwich bread I wanted. Later, by memorization, I would discover where my particular brand was. Next I went to the cooler for a gallon of milk. I knew that if I grabbed a carton of milk I could accidentally pick up chocolate milk, so I reached for a plastic jug instead. I knew from memory that bologna would be round and the other lunchmeat would be in oblong-shaped containers, so I had no problem buying bologna. I could not tell the difference in TV dinners by their boxes, but I could tell which bag of vegetables was the mixed vegetables I used for cooking. Most store managers stock the children's cereal boxes at the eye level of children which means that the other cereals are on the top shelves. I simply felt for the largest quantity of the largest boxes and was pretty well assured that they would be corn flakes. (I was usually right.)

My next stop was the meat cooler where I picked up a small package of hamburger. I was not yet experienced enough to be sure of any of the other meats except chicken.

Satisfied and rather smug, I wheeled my cart to the check out and then, just to give the checkout girl something to think about, I picked up a Reader's

Digest from the counter. I did not know what magazine I was picking up. It really didn't matter.

I had all of the money in my wallet folded different ways so I knew where the ones, five's, and tens were. As I picked up my grocery bags, I realized that there had been one thing I had not taken into account when I planned this excursion. How was I going to use my cane if I had to use both arms to carry the grocery bags? Refusing to accept defeat, I thanked God that I only lived two blocks away as I stumbled out the door. By the time I arrived home I had tripped and dropped my bags several times. I had to re-package everything myself. I was thankful that no one saw me. I again thanked God that I had not bought any eggs as I dropped my bags on the living room floor. I had done it! I had proven to myself that I could go grocery shopping alone. I still had a lot to learn about grocery shopping, but I had taken the first step and succeeded. It would have to get easier.

There were many humorous things that happened those first few months that made it easier to not only accept my situation but also to laugh at my situation. I was even able to laugh at myself.

One of the classes I took at CBC that summer was a class in homiletics. I was required to preach three times during the course, and my fellow classmates would critique my sermons. I spent many long hours working on my first sermon, because unlike the other students I was unable to use notes. I was still too slow a Braille reader, and I needed my hands to be free for gestures. The only thing I could do was to memorize my entire sermon.

I felt confident with both my sermon and my delivery as I spoke to the class. After my sermon was over and I sat down, the critiques from the other students were handed to me. Three of the students asked on their critiques why I had memorized my sermon instead of using an outline like they did. Three students did not even know that I was blind!

Once when I used the city bus to go downtown, the lady sitting across from me started telling me abut her stamp collection. I didn't realize until after I got off the bus that she thought my Braille book was a stamp album.

Most of the time when I would walk back and forth to school, I carried a large tape recorder so I could record my classes for easier studying. After I learned to walk to school without being bothered by distracting sounds, I started listening to tapes on my way to class.

To do this I used an earphone from the tape recorder to my ear. I would walk with one hand carrying my recorder and one hand using my cane. One time a young woman came up to me after watching me for some time. When she approached me she asked, "Pardon me, but have you ever found anything with your Geiger counter?" When I thought about how I must have looked to her, I laughed all the way to school.

After I had more or less become used to being blind (can anyone ever really get used to being blind?), I began to wonder seriously about my future. I was certain that I could finish school, but what would I do after I graduated? Would I be able to find work? I decided to talk to one of my teachers about the problem. I had strong respect for my teachers, and I valued their opinions.

"Sit down, Joe. What can I do for you?"

"Well, sir, I'm wondering about what I'm going to do after graduation. A degree is useless to me if no one will hire me. What chance do you think I have of making something of myself?"

"You want my honest opinion?"

"Yes, sir."

"Well, Joe, I think you should quit school. I'm sure that there's some kind of trade that some kind of blind organization can give you. You're smart, and you've got your life pretty well together, but you will never be able to preach. No minister will ever let you speak from his pulpit. And as for your drama, there is no way that you will ever be able to act as a sighted person on stage. You need to face the facts. You don't belong here. Maybe you could work with other handicapped people."

I had heard this same kind of language for two years and I was losing my patience. Why didn't anyone ever believe in me? I knew what I could do and I was determined to do it.

"Sir, I thank you for your opinion. After all, I did ask you for it." I stood and started to walk toward the door. With my hand on the doorknob I turned to face him. "Sir, there is just one more thing I want to say. I have been told for two years that I don't belong in school. Yet I have proven that I do belong in school. I have very good grades, and I have been active in several ministries. Someday I will not only play a sighted person, but I will have the lead role in a play! (Now why did I say that?) I am going to finish Bible College but I am also going to attend a state college to learn to act. It can be done and I will do it! Oh, and by the way, I'm not handicapped. I'll see you tomorrow in class. Good-bye."

It was apparent that I had not yet learned to control my emotions. After I cooled down I would go back and apologize for my actions; but I would not apologize for my words.

I did not finish the last session of summer school at CBC. I became very sick and was confined to my bed for several weeks. During that time Dana was a great friend. He did all of the cooking and even bought me a television to fill in the long, tiring days.

After I recovered, Randy Schussman, my friend from Stilltower, South Dakota, asked me to visit him in his new home in Wisconsin. I gladly accepted his offer. It felt good to be with my old friend again, and I enjoyed being back on a ranch. I had grown up surrounded by animals (I don't mean my brothers and sisters) and I enjoyed being with them again. Randy and I once again sat around his kitchen table discussing the Bible. For two beautiful weeks it felt like time had stopped, and I was once again in Stilltower, South Dakota.

While I was visiting Randy, Dana called to tell me that an unexpected check had come to me. The check was for almost $700! I had dreamed of adding on to my trailer, and now I had the money to do it.

I wanted to add on a larger living room so that I would have the room to help other people that needed a place to stay. I knew how grateful I had been when other people helped me, and now I wanted to return the kindness.

After I returned to Springfield, Dana and I started to work on the project immediately. Our first step (and the most fun) was to tear out the old dining room wall. The sound of Dana's saw cutting the metal was like music. After we had cut the outside sheet of metal and had safely taped the electrical wiring to the inside trailer walls, we put a blanket over the new hole and planned our next step.

Dana was a good carpenter, and the two of us built a platform for the new floor and walls. Dana was working full-time now and was very tired at night when he came home, but he was as excited about the addition as I was; so he spent many long hours in the evening working while I held a heavy light to help him see in the dark.

After the outside walls were up we started looking for a fireplace. I expected to pay about $300, so I was surprised to find that after I bought a fireplace and all the equipment that went with it I would spend about $500! That was far too much money for me to spend, so I was trying to figure out an alternative when a stranger approached me in the store. "Excuse me sir, but I noticed you and your friend were looking at that fireplace."

"Yes, I was. But it's too expensive for me. Besides, I wanted it in orange, and I was hoping for a larger one."

"Is that a fact?"

"Yes. Why do you ask?"

"I just happen to have an orange one. It's larger than that one and I'll sell it to you for $150."

"Wow!" (What else was there to say?)

That was how I found the perfect fireplace. God was even helping me build my addition.

The trailer originally had a booth-type dinette and I really liked it, so with a little adjusting we put it in the new room. Our next step was to put up the paneling. The trailer had very beautiful paneling, and I wanted the paneling in the new room to match it. That was a difficult task! It was very expensive paneling and it did not have a stain or finish on it. We had to do that ourselves. Dana handed me a piece of sandpaper and said, "Go to work!" One advantage to having fingers sensitive enough to read Braille is that they are also sensitive enough to feel any rough spots in the paneling. While Dana worked during the day I sanded down the paneling. Dana then put on the stain and finish. We were both very proud of his work.

The next part of the project was the hardest and the most rewarding. Especially for Dana. I had found a wall mural that I liked, and Dana decided to put it on the wall behind the fireplace. It was a picture of a forest in autumn and it covered the entire wall from floor to ceiling. It was the finishing touch to a beautiful room. I could see it very clearly in my mind.

The next part of the project I wanted to do by myself. I knew exactly how I wanted the room to look, so I set out to finish the masterpiece Dana was building. First, I bought a round braided rug and a Boston rocker for in front of the fireplace. I was very fortunate to find an old-fashioned love seat rocking chair to set beside the Boston rocker. I searched all of the second-hand stores in Springfield until I found an old wooden beer keg. (That's just what every Bible College student needs in his home!) And I filled the keg with an assortment of colorful dried leaves and set it beside the love seat. Next I had another friend build me a breakfast bar and connect it to my booth dinette. For a bench under the breakfast bar I bought a cloth-covered trunk. I finished the job by hanging dark brown curtains with fall leaves on the windows. Our masterpiece was complete!

My work on the addition was changing me in ways that I could not see. My friends tried to tell me what was happening to me, but I refused to listen. Although I had begun the work with the intention of using it to help other people in need, I was becoming so engrossed in the project that I was becoming materialistic.

I grew up in a home that had few luxuries, and I learned to be content with very little in the way of worldly goods. My father was the kind of man who was content to have a roof over his head, food in his stomach, and a book to read at bed time. He had no need for televisions, telephones, lace tablecloths, or any of the finer things of life. Because I grew up with this philosophy, it was easy for me to be content with very little.

But now that was changing. The more possessions I owned, the more I wanted. I could not satisfy my need for "things." For the first time in my life I was in a position to have a few nice things and I wanted to take full advantage of the situation. As soon as I would finish one project on the trailer I would start another.

At about the same time that Dana finished the construction of my room addition and moved into his own apartment, school began. I had decided that I would not return to CBC for the fall semester. Instead, I would attend Southwest Missouri State University. I wanted to take some drama courses, and I wanted to compete with students that had more of a background in drama than I did. That step was the first in a series that would change my life forever.

EIGHT

A state college is very different from a Bible college. There are the obvious differences like the dress code and the names of the classes. But there are subtle differences also; like humanism and existentialism, philosophies that try to challenge the basic core of Christianity. Those ideas are prevalent in a secular state college. But it is those very philosophies that make a state college such a challenge to the lifestyle and beliefs of a Christian.

It took a lot of pleading, but my advisor finally let me enroll in some drama courses. One course was drama history, and I was to have had at least two years of drama theory as a prerequisite. The instructor let me in anyway. I had two communication courses and one science class. The rest of my classes were drama courses. I learned immediately that it can be very difficult for a Christian in

a state college. My drama instructor required me to do several activities that I refused to do because I was a Christian.

"But you have to do these things in order to complete the course. They are required!"

"Then flunk me! Look, I don't want to cause any trouble, but I am a Christian, and I will not participate in these activities. I need the class in order to graduate, but if my not participating means that you will flunk me, then I have no choice but to flunk. The decision is up to you."

I stayed in the class, and I was able to choose the activities I participated in. Because of my stand it was soon known all over campus that I was a Christian. It meant that I had to constantly be aware of my actions, but it was a good experience. I knew that people were looking at me first, not as a blind man, but as a Christian. At the end of the semester I asked my drama instructor if she thought that I had any potential as an actor.

"Joe, I like you, so I'm going to be honest with you. Some people have the ability to act, and some people have the ability to act like they're acting, but Joe, you have neither! Maybe you should quit school and learn a trade."

There it was again! The more everyone told me to quit school, the more determined I became to make it through school.

My favorite class that semester was not one of my drama classes. It was my science class, "The Inhabited Earth."

The professor was the most pessimistic person I had ever known. He was certain that the world would end in five years. He saw no hope for the future of planet earth. He believed strongly in Darwinism, and I enjoyed challenging his statements about evolution. The day before the final exam I stopped by his office.

"Sir, can I see you for a minute?"

"Sure. Come on in."

"I want to talk to you about the final test tomorrow."

"Well, Joe, you shouldn't have much trouble with the test. I know that you pay attention in class. I can give you the test orally myself."

"Sir, that's not the problem. I know all the answers to the test. I've studied a lot, and I have no problem there. It's just that you want me to write down answers that agree with Darwinism and evolution, and I won't do that. The answers that you want me to write on the test aren't really the true answers."

"Joe, I'll make you a deal. I know that you're a Christian. If you can scientifically prove to me, without using your Bible, that Darwinism does not exist then I will give you an "A" for the class and you won't have to take the final test."

I got an "A" for the class.

I was beginning to open myself up more to other people now. I had been afraid of trying to start a relationship with any of the young ladies I knew. I did not want to lose anyone again as I had lost Jami. The only young lady that had been in my life since I lost Jami was Michelle, and we were only friends.

Then I met Angie. Her father was the pastor of a small church a few blocks from my home. We started spending our school lunch hours together. It soon became my favorite part of the day. Angie was the first person I had met after losing my sight that did not seem to care whether I could see or not. We enjoyed being with each other and that was all that mattered to either of us. After talking to each other over hamburgers for three weeks, I finally asked her out.

"Well, Joe, where do you want to go?"

"I don't know. I feel like doing something really crazy. Something that a blind person would never think of doing."

"How about going roller skating?"

"But I have never been on skates in my life!"

"Then it's about time you learned what you've been missing!"

We knew that if I went in using a white cane the manager would never let me out on the roller rink. That is why we walked in arm in arm. She was able to lead me and no one else could see what she was really doing. We looked just like any other couple on the skating floor.

I was nervous about what to do but of course I could not let Angie know that! We rented our skates and I could feel my heart beat faster as I put them on. Then we walked out to the skating floor. (Joe, what in the world are you getting yourself into? You're not only going to break your neck, but you'll probably hurt somebody else as well!) I smiled as I told Angie that I wasn't worried. We stepped onto the floor.

She gave me a push and off I went! I had no idea of what to do, and I needed to spend all of my energy just concentrating on standing up. I grabbed hold of the railing and walked along the outside wall until I had walked around the arena twice.

I could hear the other skaters so I knew whenever I was near someone. I skated with both arms stretched out as far as I could reach. That served two purposes. First, it helped me to keep my balance and second, it let everyone else know that I had never been on skates so they stayed away from me.

We had a beautiful evening, and by the time the roller rink closed, I was skating like I had at least some idea of what I was doing. Amazingly, I never fell the entire night. If I would have fallen, I doubt that I would have been able to get up again.

We were both very quiet as she parked the car in front of my trailer.

"What's wrong Joe? I've never seen you so quiet."

"I was just thinking."

"That usually means trouble!"

"Ya', probably. You know, Angie, I had a lot of fun tonight."

"So did I."

"But I don't think we should go out again."

"But why? You just said you had fun."

"I know but it's just that… Well, Angie, we like each other. A lot. And this could lead to something nice, but I don't think that either of us wants that. I'm blind. It would never work between us."

"Yes, it would. I don't care if you're blind."

"I know, but later you would. Right now the idea of loving a blind man is romantic. Something like you would see on TV. But later the excitement would wear off, and I would start to depend too much on you, and you would start to resent it."

"There's something you're not telling me. What is it?"

"You know, you sound like someone I used to know when you say that. But you're right. There is something else that's bothering me. I don't know if I can explain it.

"When I first started to go blind, I decided that I would never act blind. I wanted sympathy from no one. I knew what people expected blind people to act like and I refused to fill the stenotype. I wanted to stay in a seeing world. I thought that somehow if I didn't act blind then no one else would think of me as blind.

"I want to stay in a seeing world, and I can't. I don't want to be part of a blind world, but I have no choice. It isn't like it would be if I were born blind. Then I would easily belong to a blind world. I'm part of both worlds, and at the same time I'm not comfortable in either world. I can't make any lasting decisions until I know where I belong."

"It is best to end our relationship now, before it goes any farther. It will save us both a lot of pain later on. I know what I'm doing, and I'm right. Goodnight, Angie."

I kissed her on the cheek and was halfway to my front door before I heard her say, "Good-bye Joe."

After that I spent little time with socializing. I spent most of my time working on my trailer. That fall a friend and I built a rather elaborate greenhouse on the front of my trailer. As soon as it was complete, I furnished it with living room furniture and as many plants as I could find. Aside from being a luxury, it was rather practical. It cut my heating costs down considerably. Even with my fireplace in the addition I still needed another source of heat. A friend from church built me a wood burning furnace for my living room to replace the one that smoked so badly. The new one still smoked the place up quite a bit, but it was much more efficient than the first stove had been.

When I started school at Southwest Missouri State University, I also started going to a church Dana introduced me to. It was an exciting church, and it was unusual in many ways. The church had started as a Bible study a few years earlier, and as God blessed the church it grew. The congregation was almost all students, so we had a lot in common with each other.

It was through this church that I started my drama ministry. Dana and I did a few skits one night at the church, and the response was great. From that

I was asked to perform in concert with a local group as a "special guest appearance by Joe Ransom."

I was really excited! It was the first time since I had become a Christian that people actually paid to see me act. Between songs from the band, I did several skits with friends. Then as my final number I did a solo drama called "Phone Call From God".

It was an evening I will never forget. I choreographed the skits myself, and since there was very little body movement involved, it wasn't difficult to act like I could see. I rehearsed all of the skits several times on stage before the concert, and I counted all of my steps so that I knew exactly how far I was to move for every action I was to do. That night proved to me that with a lot of practice I would be able to perform complicated interactions with other people on stage. (Yes sir, Joe! Someday you will have the lead in a play. I'm sure of it!)

As Christmas approached I began to have the "Holiday Season Blues." The holidays had always been a sad time for me. Christmas is meant to be spent with family and friends, but I had had to spend Christmas by myself for many years. I was lonely, and I needed to do something to change my feeling about Christmas.

I thought about all of the different attitudes toward Christmas that I was seeing around me. From those attitudes I wrote a small play titled "The Penetrating Question." It was a comedy with a very serious message. It was fun to direct the play at Christian Life Center in Springfield at Christmas time. The play did more than simply lift my spirit. It reminded me of the true meaning of Christmas.

That play showed me that with a lot of work and even more patience I could direct a play. I had to admit that my methods were rather unorthodox but at least they worked. I directed the play from several rows back in the audience. I relied almost entirely on my hearing, so I was determined to hear them perfectly. I had trained myself to distinguish the direction a person was facing by listening to him speak. After a lot of practice I was able to tell who was blocking (in the way of) another actor.

About the only thing that I could not "see" with sound was facial expression on the cast members. If I wanted to check the facial expression on someone, I would yell "Freeze" and everyone would freeze their expressions and their positions on stage. I would then go on stage, and, by using my hands, I would feel the expressions on their faces. The first time I did this resulted in laughter from the actors, but after that everyone obeyed my order to freeze and everything went more smoothly.

It was thrilling on the night of the performance to sit in the audience and "watch" a play's being performed that I had written and directed. At the end of the production as I sat on the stage and listened to the quiet all around me, I bowed my head in thanksgiving to God for fulfilling my dreams as I dedicated that building to be used for Christian drama. (Editor's Note: Today that building is the Stained Glass Theatre, Missouri's first full time Christian theatre.)

In January I felt that it was finally time for me to go to Evangel College. I had not yet finished Bible College, but I was planning to return to CBC in September. I wanted a degree in drama, and it looked as though Evangel had what I wanted.

I had not been on the Evangel campus since that night one year earlier when God had told me that someday this would be my school. I spent two days before classes started walking around campus picturing everything in my mind and memorizing where everything was located. By the time the students started returning from Christmas break I knew the campus well enough to walk around blindfolded!

Time passed and school continued. It was a busy time for me because I was also spending time at the Association for the Blind. Many times I would leave home at 7:00 a.m. and not return until after midnight. It was only with the help of Dr. Dalan, the drama director, that I managed to survive the semester. Most of my classes were with her, and she tutored me herself. I will never be able to thank her enough for all her help. Not only did she tutor me, she also insisted on feeding me. It wasn't hard for her to guess that the only time I ate well was when she fed me.

As the long, cold winter progressed, we had the biggest snowfall in Springfield's history. I loved it, at first. Then I started thinking about my poor trailer, because I knew the roof could not handle the weight of the snow. I had to get on the roof (no easy task) and sweep the snow off before the snow's weight caved it in.

I took a kitchen chair and broom and started walking with them through the snow. (Oops, I bumped into the greenhouse. Watch where you're going, Joe.) I slipped in the snow, picked up the chair and broom, and continued to walk to the back of the trailer. The back of the trailer was curved to the roof, so it would be the easiest part to climb. As I adjusted the chair under the license plate I was struck by the humor of the situation. The snow had completely covered the back of the trailer, and as I cleared it away, I remembered that the license plate I was clearing off said "California." I would love to have had a picture of my snow-bound home with its California license.

Every attempt to climb the trailer failed. The trailer back was iced over and I would simply slide down. Finally, I threw the broom onto the roof. Then, standing on the chair, I took a giant leap and grabbed the edge of the roof. I prayed 'Lord, don't let me fall," as I pulled myself up onto the roof. (Whew! I don't know how I'll get down, but at least I'm up here.)

I was really enjoying my work. I would sweep the snow off the roof and then I would sweep it off the greenhouse. As I stepped to the greenhouse, I misjudged the distance by only one step. That's all it took. I slipped onto the greenhouse roof and rolled off the roof onto the ground. (Thanks, Lord, for all this snow to break my fall.) I did, however, tear the ligaments in my foot and twist my ankle. Again, the situation was too funny for me to stay angry very long. I could picture what I would look like as I walked to school. I wore a heavy backpack to carry my tape recorder and Braille typewriter to school. As I walked to school on crutches, I used the thumb and forefinger on my left hand to maneuver my white cane. It is not easy to walk with crutches and a white cane in three feet of snow. One time, one of my friends drove past me on my way to school. He was so surprised at the sight that he turned to stare at me and drove his car into a snow bank.

I was sitting in Dr. Dalan's office one afternoon discussing what I would do for a certain drama project. Suddenly her phone rang.

"Dr. Dalan here. You want to know if I know of someone that could play the lead in Tartuffe? Yes,

I do know of someone. Yes, I'll send him right down. His name is Joe Ransom, and he's in my office now. Thank you, good-bye."

"Well, I've solved your problem. For your next project you're going to play the lead in a French play. The play is a classic."

"But I don't speak French! And you didn't tell him I'm blind! He's not gonna want a blind guy that doesn't speak French to have the lead in his play. Who is the director, anyway?"

"I am sure that the director is not going to care whether or not you speak French. And "he" is a she. Her name is Mrs. Jones."

Oh, well. At least she doesn't sound French.

"That's fine, but who is she?"

"The French teacher."

I had to ask, didn't I?

Evangel's French department wanted to do something different from the usual for their project this year. They decided to perform a French drama but they had no one to play the lead, so they asked Dr. Dalan if she could recommend someone to them.

That was how I came to be sitting in a French classroom listening to French students read a French play to a French teacher.

"You must be Joe Ransom. I'm the French teacher, Mrs. Jones. Have a seat. We're reading a play by Moliere. Are you familiar with Moliere?"

"No, Ma'am. I don't speak French."

"Oh. Well, the play we will be doing is a play by Moliere. Did Dr. Dalan tell you that?"

"No, Ma'am. She just told me you were doing a French play and wanted me to play a man named Tartuffe."

"Don't look so worried. We'll be doing an English translation of the play. You won't have to speak French."

"Ma'am?"

"Yes?"

"What did Dr. Dalan tell you about me?"

"She said you had quite a bit of theatre in your background. That is about all she said. Why?"

"Well, Ma'am. I don't want to ruin your plans or anything but I'm uh, well, you see, I'm blind."

"Oh. Well, that will make it more interesting!"

(Bless her heart!)

"We will start rehearsing next week."

And so we did. It took me longer to learn my lines than it did most of the rest of the cast. It was not because I had more lines to memorize; it was just that I had to memorize my lines from a tape recorder.

If memorizing lines was difficult, rehearsing the actions on stage was nearly impossible. We had to do everything but nail down the furniture in order to keep me from tripping on it. After several months of practice, I was able to move around the furniture fairly easily, but it was rather difficult for me to do intricate movements like pouring wine into a glass or grabbing an apple from the fruit bowl without grabbing a pear instead.

As the days passed I grew more confident of my ability. I was thankful that the play was a comedy. That way, if I did make a mistake on stage, it would be easier for me to cover it up without letting the audience know what happened.

As fate had it, I was not fortunate enough to be on my deathbed the night of the performance. Still, I did manage to spend the entire first act (my opening appearance was in act two) in the men's room backstage. And boy, was I sick! This was to be my final test. This night would tell me once and for all whether I had the ability to act. Playing Tartuffe was difficult, but playing sighted was nearly impossible!

After I had been on stage for a few minutes I began to relax and even started to enjoy myself. But my new found courage was short lived. At one point in the play I was to attempt to seduce another man's wife. I was down on my knees, and she was lying on the couch. As I stood up I realized that in front of the audience I was losing my pants! (Fortunately I was wearing a long black gown over my shirt.) I grabbed for my waist and spent the rest of the scene with my fists clenching the waistband of my pants. Luckily, the only people that noticed something was wrong were the people who had read the script. I was able to improvise until the end of the scene when I dashed backstage to find a safety pin. Now I know why it is called a safety pin!

It was the next scene, however, that almost destroyed me. I was again trying to seduce the same woman, and to my declaration of love for her she said, "But what if I tell my husband?" My response was, "But I know you will forgive my temerity, and you will see that when I look at you, I see, that is, well, after all, I'm not blind!" Those in the audience that did not know me did not see the irony. The line was not meant to be funny. But from the back of the audience I heard a roar of laughter from my friends. I almost lost control of the situation but with improvisation I finished the scene.

After the play was over and the audience had gone on to other things, I was left alone with my thoughts. I remembered the afternoon in my teacher's office at CBC when I told him I would have the lead in a play. I remembered my drama instructor at SMSU telling me that I would never act. And I remembered the night in California when God told me that I would use drama to minister. God is so faithful! With Him, truly, all things are possible. My dream had begun and nothing would ever stop it.

NINE

Like most of the important and life-changing days of our lives, that day began as all others. It was February 29, 1980. I went through my day of classes as if it were any normal day. Tomorrow would be the last day of classes before spring break at Evangel, and I was planning my days of study and relaxation ahead of me. After tomorrow I would have 10 beautiful days to enjoy my remodeled home. The added room was finished, and the greenhouse had been completed the week before. Ten beautiful days to relax and enjoy. Or so I thought.

I checked the fire in the furnace, turned off the TV, and went to bed. (Tonight I can go to sleep and not worry about getting up in the morning. This is Heaven!) I had been in bed for about an hour when suddenly I was wide-awake. I had no reason to wake up so suddenly, so I thought the Lord must have had a reason to wake me.

As soon as I walked into the living room, I knew why God had awakened me. On the ceiling, above the furnace was a small fire. I could feel the heat and I could hear it burning. It was nothing to get excited about. I grabbed a kettle from under the sink and started to fill it with water when suddenly there was an explosion and the entire front end of my trailer was in flames. I was standing in the middle of an inferno! The front door had completely disintegrated. I knew that I could not put out the fire and I needed to find a way out of the trailer, fast!

There were several more explosions and the trailer was completely engulfed in flames. It is amazing what the Christian thinks about at a time like that. I had perfect calm, and at no time did I panic. Two verses of scripture came to mind. The first was from Isaiah: "When thou walkest through the fire, thou shalt not be burned; neither shall the flame kindle upon thee." The second was from Job: "The Lord gave, and the Lord hath taken away; blessed be the name of the Lord." I knew that only two things could happen; I would either be saved from the fire and live to tell of God's goodness, or I would die and go to Heaven. Either way I would win. But I also knew that if I stayed in the trailer, I would be committing suicide and that would be wrong.

My only chance for escape was to go through the bedroom door and break out through the greenhouse. As I entered the smoke-filled bedroom, I grabbed a shirt and a pair of pants just before my closet fell to the floor in cinders. As I entered the greenhouse, I was almost overcome by smoke. Because the greenhouse was airtight, it had more smoke in it than did the trailer. I knew that the smoke would kill me long before the fire would, and I dashed back into the trailer for air. I stuck my head under what was left of the blankets on my bed. I prayed a quick "God give me an idea" as I ran back to the greenhouse. I held my breath as I grabbed a stool and tried to break through five layers of plexiglass. I tried to ignore the explosions behind me and the falling timbers around me as I hammered my way to safety. As soon as I was able to make a small hole in the wall, I dived through it just as an explosion completely destroyed the spot where I had been standing.

The first thing I did was to get on my knees and thank God for saving me and thank Him for the lessons I would learn from the fire. Some may say that the fire could not have come from God, but later I would see that next to my salvation, that fire was the best thing to ever happen to me! As I stood barefoot in the snow I knew that if I could see, I would be watching everything I owned go up in smoke. I did not know why it happened, but I knew that God knew and that was all that mattered. God had everything under control. Later, even the fire chief said it was a miracle. No one could have lived through that fire and yet not one hair on my head was singed!

It took half an hour for the fire department to get to the trailer and by then the only thing they could do was try to keep the fire from spreading to other trailers.

A stranger approached me and asked me how I felt. I told him that if I were not a Christian, I would be feeling pretty miserable, but because I was a Christian I had nothing to worry about. I learned the next morning that the stranger had been a reporter with a tape recorder as I heard our conversation over the radio.

Within minutes after the fire, God began showing me things he wanted me to learn. One of the men that had stayed in my trailer was now my next-door neighbor. I spent the night at his place. The pillow, bedding, and towels I used were the ones I had given him when he moved out of my place. (Later Dana would give me back the dishes I had given him when he moved into his own apartment.) The only things I had saved were the things I had given away!

My first phone call the next morning was to Dana. I knew he would be hurt by the fire, and I wanted to try to find an easy way to tell him about it.

"Hello?"

"Dana?"

"Ya'."

"Dana, this is Joe. Remember that wall mural of the forest you made for me?"

"Ya'. What about it?"

"Well, Dana, we had a forest fire."

After I told Evangel about the fire, they did everything they could to help me. It was the last morning before break, so very few students were in chapel that day. When the chapel speaker announced that I had been burned out, the students gave me a love offering of several hundred dollars. One of my classes even took up an extra offering for me. A married couple gave me the use of their apartment while they were on spring break. Students from Evangel and CBC donated clothes, pots and pans, bedding and everything they could find to help me out.

Other help came from churches and people in the community. People were very good to me, and it served as a real morale booster to find that truly genuine and helpful people do care and can still be found.

The first thing for me to do was to find a permanent place to stay, but before I did that I needed to go back to the trailer. Ted, a friend from Evangel, and I talked about God's goodness as he drove me to what was left of my home.

As I walked through the rubble of my dream, God spoke to me. He told me that He would replace everything I had lost or show me that I did not need it in the first place. And as God spoke to me He showed me His sense of humor.

Inside the cloth-covered trunk I had used for a bench under the breakfast nook I had put $30 worth of fire logs for my fireplace. After the fire everything was gone, even the trunk, but there was a neat pile of fire logs! The things that were to light with a little match didn't burn.

Earlier that morning I found that all but one of my school books could be replaced. My biology book was out of stock. As I walked through the rubble I found that out of hundreds of books, one book had apparently lifted itself off the bookshelf and jumped through a closed window. It didn't even get wet by the fire hoses. It was my biology book.

My Braille typewriter had been in a metal case and the case had melted, but the typewriter was unharmed even though the keys were plastic and the bottom was cardboard. God knew that it would take me several months to order a new one, and I could not afford the time to wait.

I did not know until months later, but the night of the fire some of my friends had been talking and one of them had said, "You know, it may not be nice to say, but I hope Joe's trailer burns down. He's gotten to the point that his trailer is his god, and God can't talk to him anymore." It is not sad that he said it; it is sad that it was true.

Another friend from church later told me that a week before the fire she had had a dream that my trailer would burn, but she had been afraid to say anything to me. I told her that if she ever had a dream like that again to please give me a week's notice.

The biggest lesson I was to learn was that if it would tear you apart to lose something material, it means too much to you. People are to be loved, things are to be used; not the other way around. If you own something, give it back to God. He gave it to you in the first place and if He wants it, He could take it away. They are just things and in the light of eternity they don't make any difference.

But as many lessons are learned through pain and sorrow, this one also had a price. As I walked through the snow-covered rubble, I pushed my hands against the sides of the trailer in an attempt to find something familiar. I tripped and fell to my knees. The wind was whistling as I found it lying in the snow. It had been a picture of my mother, taken many years ago. All that was left was a broken and charred frame. I sat on the snow and felt the warm tears trickle down my face as my mind went back to other days.

I remembered my mother's funeral when I was in the first grade.

And I remembered my first girl friend; she was six and I was seven. Her name was Claudia.

I remembered horseback rides and mountain lakes.

And I remembered Grandpa's funeral.

I remembered the night I became a Christian.

I remembered my father's coming backstage after our high school production of Charlie's Aunt just to tell me he was proud of me.

And I remembered Jami.

As I slowly stood to leave, I knew that I was saying good-bye to a part of me that would never be seen again. As I said good-bye to my memories and walked away to start a new life, I knew that in 20 minutes a boy became a man.

TEN

After walking away from the rubble for the last time Ted and I went apartment shopping. I had two requirements: first that it be cheap, and second, that it be furnished.

By late afternoon I found the apartment I wanted. It was very large although it had only two bedrooms. The living room had beautiful French doors dividing it from the rest of the apartment. With it's high ceilings I felt like I was in a ballroom. Its overstuffed furniture gave it the feeling of "Grandma's house." Best of all was the price; fully furnished and utilities included for only $175 per month.

I had somewhat of a problem though when I went to talk to the manager.

"Mr. Ransom, how long will it take you to move in?"

"Oh, about 30 seconds."

"Huh?"

"Well, sir, I guess you could say I travel light."

"Huh?"

He was a great conversationalist.

"I don't have any clothes or bedding or kitchen utensils, or anything."

"How are you going to live?"

"God will give me what I need."

"I don't follow you."

And so it was that I told him about the fire. Since I had already signed the lease, he reluctantly let me move in.

With the help of my family and friends it took less than one month for my new apartment to become as crowded as my trailer had been.

People from all over Springfield were cleaning out their attics and bringing me their garage sale items. Thanks to the kindness and love of many people, I had a new home.

As summer drew to a close, I began to feel homesick for my friends and family in Tacoma, Washington. I had not seen any of them since the year before I left for college. I spent two beautiful weeks back home. I was closer to my little brother and two sisters during those weeks than I had ever been. We did not discuss my blindness. There was no need to. Words will never express the joy I felt at once again being with Pastor Bennett and Pastor Bulluck who had led and directed me as a baby Christian.

As the time passed, God continued opening doors for me to speak and witness of His love and goodness. After speaking in Evangel's chapel service one morning, Katrinka Sawin interviewed me and wrote an article for Vision, a publication from Evangel. One time I spoke to a group of campers in Arkansas. The more I shared of what God had done in my life, the more I wanted to share of what He was doing.

I started to think about opening my home again to those in need of a place to stay. This time, however, it was for better motives than it had been with my trailer. God had blessed me, and I wanted to share that blessing with others. That is how Joe Teeter came to stay with me. Now, let me explain Joe Teeter.

Earlier that fall I met Joe Teeter, who would become another close friend. My church was going on a caving expedition, and Joe was an experienced caver; so he decided to come with us. He and I were put together as partners.

Although I had never been in a cave, I had a distinct advantage over the others in the group; I knew how to walk in the dark. So, it seemed natural to me that I take the lead. If I knew then what I now know (thanks to Joe Teeter) about caving, I would never have attempted such a stunt. Only an experienced caver should ever lead a caving expedition. Not only was it wrong for me to attempt to lead the group, but I acted cocky as I did it. I was trying too hard to prove to everyone that a blind person can do anything he wants to do. I was doing as a blind person what even a sighted person should not do.

It was several months before I saw Joe Teeter again. When I did see him again, I could not remember his first name. For some unknown reason it took me about three weeks before I could remember his name. By the time that I had his name firmly implanted in my memory, we were already becoming known as the "Two Musketeers" on campus. Joe and I became fast friends, and the reason was simple. Joe never made allowances for my blindness. It wasn't that he ignored my blindness; he just didn't see it. Everything he did, he assumed I could do.

It was Joe Teeter who took me on my first "blind date." He and his girl friend had been working on the stereo at my place when I suggested that we go out to eat. They both liked the idea but thought that I should have a date. Whom would I ask? I had no girl friends, and I knew no one that was willing to date a blind man. Joe's girl friend had an idea.

"Let's ask my roommate Carol if she will go out with you."

"But she's never seen me, and she won't want to go out with a blind man."

"We won't tell her you're blind. We'll just ask her if she wants to go on a 'blind date.'"

And so we did.

I had to plan the evening very carefully. I did not want Carol to know that I was blind until I thought it was the proper time. First, I would have to leave my cane at home. That was a dead giveaway. Second, we would have to eat at a pizza parlor because you don't use silverware with pizza, and no one notices if you're messy. Third, we would go to a movie after the pizza. After all, what can go wrong at a theater? And fourth, Joe Teeter would have to wear his key chain. Joe had a loud set of keys, and I could easily follow him when they jingled.

Everything started out as planned. We picked up Carol at her dorm and Joe drove us to the pizza parlor. But as we got out of the car I realized that Joe was not wearing his keys! Joe caught the problem and in order to compensate he told the girls to be careful not to run into the curb in front of them. By telling them, he was telling me.

Things went smoothly once inside the pizza parlor. As we were leaving, Joe noticed that the theatre we planned to go to was farther away than he had originally thought. It was to my advantage that the ground was covered with snow and ice. I told Carol that we should walk arm in arm so she would not slip on the ice. By doing so she could lead me without knowing it.

After the movie was over and we were walking back to the car, Carol slipped on the ice. I told her that she should watch where she was going. Because of the situation, Joe, his girl friend and I started laughing. It really wasn't that funny. It was just that the "secret" we were keeping from Carol made us tense. Of course, Carol didn't see the humor and decided that she should go back to her dorm.

Many people have asked me how I could be so cruel as to keep my blindness a secret from my date. I wasn't trying to be cruel; I was simply trying to prove a point. I wanted to be liked or disliked because of my personality, not because of my blindness. Few girls would ever consider dating a blind man, and of those I did date, most patronized me. They dated me because they felt sorry for me or because no one else would date them. They assumed that if they couldn't get a date and I couldn't get a date that we would make a good couple. One girl I dated insisted on ruining the movie by describing every minute detail to me. She even told me that Kermit the frog was green.

Actually, I did plan to tell Carol that I was blind. I just wanted to give her a chance to know me as a person first. However, I never had the opportunity to tell her. After we stopped at her dorm on the way home, she got out of the car before I had a chance to tell her. Later that night when she told her friends about me, they told her I was blind. It was quite some time before she let me get close enough to her to apologize and explain my reasons for what I had done.

Because Joe and I had the same interests, we spent a lot of time together. He would tease me about my blindness but because it was all "in fun," I enjoyed it. More than once he took my cane from me and made me chase him to get it back. To the other students on campus, it probably looked like he was being mean to me, but that never bothered him. And it never bothered me.

As we were walking around campus one day, he explained his feeling to me.

"You know, Ransom, you're not like other blind people."

"How do you mean?"

"Well, you trip on the sidewalk and run into walls occasionally, but other than that you don't act like you can't see. That's it! You're not really blind, you just can't see!"

"Hmm. Catchy title for a book, don't you think?"

After Joe Teeter moved in, another friend of his came to stay, and my apartment became rather crowded, so I started looking for a larger place to live.

About the time Joe moved out to get married and his friend moved out to go back to Texas, I found the place I was looking for. And it was in my own back yard! It was the biggest home I had ever lived in. Downstairs was a living room, parlor, kitchen with a dining table large enough to seat the Waltons, front porch and enclosed back porch. At the top of the winding staircase were three bedrooms, one of which I used for a study, and an old-fashioned bathroom, complete with claw-footed tub. And the rent was less than I was paying for my apartment. In less than a week I found two Evangel students to spend the summer with me in my new home.

As summer ended they decided to move back into the dorms on campus, and once again I was living by myself. I enjoyed my home, but with my only income being a social security check, I decided to look for a used trailer house to buy. Renting was just too expensive.

I called a friend from my former trailer court and asked her if she knew of any trailers for sale. She didn't know of any but would do some looking and call me back if she found anything. She called me back in 20 minutes.

"Joe, I think I've found the perfect trailer for you!"

"You have?"

"Yes! It's small, it's old, and it's very run down, but the owner said it's livable, and he will sell it to you for $750 unfurnished!"

"I'll tell you what. Call him back and if he will sell it to me for $500 furnished, I'll buy it."

I moved in immediately.

When my friends saw the trailer, they told me I was crazy to move in. It was true that my definition of "livable" and the owner's definition of "livable" were not the same. Rain poured through the roof, the ceiling was gone, the walls were destroyed, there was a hole in the floor where the hallway had been, the electrical wiring had been burned, and the water pipes were broken. Other than that, the trailer was in great shape!

My blindness was a real asset to me. My friends only saw the trailer for what it was, but with my imagination I saw it, as it would become. Besides,

I really had no choice but to buy the trailer; I could not afford even a cheap apartment.

The trailer had been used as a storage shed by the previous owner, and it was so full of old material that it took me three days to dig my way to the back bedroom.

The more that my friends told me I was foolish for buying the trailer, the more determined I became to make it presentable. I had no intentions of making the trailer into a fancy home as I had done with my other trailer. I only wanted to make a livable home for myself and others that might need a roof over their heads.

Shortly after I moved in, school began. I decided to return to CBC and finish the work on my Bible degree. As I stood in one of those endless registration lines that all students are familiar with, I struck up a conversation with the student in front of me. It was the beginning of a very special friendship. He told me that his name was Rick Knoth and he was from Adrian, Michigan. His roommate, Ric Muck, was also from Adrian. Rick had graduated from college and was returning for a Bible degree. Rick and Ric and I became fast friends. I will never forget Rick's first impression of my trailer. He drove me home from school the day we met, and I invited him in to see my home. I don't think he had ever seen such a disaster in his life. He wanted to be polite but couldn't think of anything nice to say. Finally he said, "Well, it's homey."

Ric Muck was several years younger than his roommate, and in many ways he reminded me of myself when I first became a Christian. He was full of excitement and zeal. He is probably the most energetic and alive person that I have ever met. And, fortunate for me, he had a problem. Ric needed a job.

And I sure had a job for him! Ric would do the primary rebuilding of my trailer. Ric, along with two of his friends, Robert Stien and Dwight Huber, performed a labor of love that not only transformed my trailer but transformed me as well. Ric spent every spare moment, and many that he couldn't spare, at my place. He put up a ceiling, put up walls, re-did the electrical wiring, spent many long hours with his crew putting in new plumbing, and did a host of other jobs too numerous to mention.

By Thanksgiving Day the trailer was far from complete, but it could boast a new ceiling, new walls, and working plumbing. I spent Thanksgiving Day with friends at the home of Dana Calef and his new wife, but before I left my trailer that day I painted the entire trailer on the inside. I probably missed a lot of spots, but since I put on three coats of paint, I figured that the spots I missed the first or second time, I painted the third time around.

I had a lot to be thankful for that day. I had a warm home, friends, food in the cupboards, and I was fortunate enough to be a student at two Christian colleges. It was the most beautiful Thanksgiving I have ever had.

After Ric returned from the Thanksgiving break he once again returned to work on the trailer. I knew how much he needed the little bit of money I paid him, but he used most of it to buy groceries for me. He was more concerned about me than I was myself. Everything he did, he did because the love of Jesus flowed through him. I really envied him because he never had any problems in his life. Or so I thought!

As he dropped me off at home one afternoon he turned to me and said, "What gives Joe? What's bugging you?"

"Forget it Ric, you wouldn't understand."

"Try me."

"It's just that everything always goes right for you. You never have any serious problems. I don't see why things can't be that way for me. I mean, most of the time I'm really thankful. I have a roof over my head and food in my stomach."

"But I'm tired of living the way I do. I never know from one day to the next where my next meal is going to come from. I'm tired of not having a family to spend time with. I'm walking 10 miles a day to school and back and I don't like it. And I don't like being blind! I want to be able to watch the trees change color in the fall, and I want to ride a bicycle and, well, I want to be like everyone else! I want to be like you."

Ric was quiet for a minute and then he put his hand on mine. I started to cry as I had never cried. After I had finished crying and had dried my eyes with apologies, Ric started to tell me his story.

"Joe, things aren't as easy for me as you think. My parents went through a divorce and it hurt me a lot. It hurt because I love both of them very much, and I don't understand how it could happen. My mother is very sick, and she's confined to the house. My brother and I have to take care of her and the house all the time. And my brother is barely in high school. I worry about them, and I want to be with Mom all the time, but I know that I can't be because God wants me here at CBC right now."

"And you know, Joe, there are times when I wish I could be like you."

"Wh-what do you mean!"

"For you, school is easy. You don't have to work at it the way I do. I have to really work to get the grades you get without trying."

"But Ric, if you have problems like that, why doesn't it ever get you down?"

"Joe, I learned something a long time ago. I have to take things one day at a time. That's all Jesus asks of me. And things do get me down sometimes, but when they do, I pray about them and let God handle the problem. When I do, He takes care of everything."

"Joe, you've been trying to solve all your problems by yourself so everyone will think you can handle any situation. But we know better. I don't know why things turned out this way for you but God does, and you know He has the answers to your problems. He will help you but only if you let Him."

I mumbled a "thank you" and turned to walk in to the trailer. Suddenly, I heard him turn and say; "I love you, brother."

I love you, brother! It had been a long, long, time since anyone had told me they loved me. But Ric loves me! God loved me, and Ric loved me. And I knew that Rick and Dana and Joe and a lot of other people loved me too. They showed me in a hundred ways every day. Truly, I was a rich man!

It was with a new perspective on myself that I went back to work on the trailer.

My most beautiful memory of that final semester at CBC came one Friday night when in a church service on campus, it was announced that Rich Knoth and Ric Muck were among the 11 students chosen from CBC to work as missionaries for the summer. I was very proud of both of them, and I knew that as they yielded their lives to God He would do great things through them.

But the real beauty of the night revealed itself to me after the service. Rick Knoth drove me home and as I entered the trailer I heard a chorus of "Happy Birthday"!!! Rick and Ric and all of the students that had worked on my trailer were throwing me a surprise party. It was so like them. When they should have been out celebrating their own victory for the night, they chose instead to be a blessing to me. With a frozen cake and warm pop, I had the best birthday of my life.

That night was the first time Rich Knoth had seen the inside of my trailer since that first day of school when he brought me home. Remembering his first description of my trailer, I asked him what he thought of the transformation in my home. He looked at the new ceiling, new walls, and new furniture, turned to me and said, "Well, it's homey."

ELEVEN

Christmas came and went. School started again in January, and I was once again back at Evangel. I had finished the work on my Bible degree at CBC, and I was now going to finish my drama degree (the official title of the degree was Communications).

My biggest obstacle that semester was a teacher named David Smith. He was a new drama director. Mr. Smith had one great fault: He was unbearably honest. Mr. Smith had one great virtue: He was unbearably honest.

From the first time we met, I knew I was facing a challenge. It was easy to see that I was going to have to impress him with my great theatrical talent! He was hard to impress.

He was directing a play that semester titled You Can't Take It With You, and I was determined to have a part in the action. He couldn't think of a specific job for me, so I decided to go to work on my own. He finally gave me a title (something like "properties man") and sent me on my way. I spent every spare minute I had hunting in secondhand stores, garage sales, and bargain basements looking for props for the play.

My real break came one night during rehearsal. He and I were sitting next to each other listening to the cast when I commented that someone was mispronouncing a word. Because Mr. Smith was so involved in reading the script, he did not catch the mistake. He immediately gave me a new job. Starting that night I would sit in the rehearsals and, using my Braille typewriter, write down all of the mistakes I heard. After rehearsal I would compliment and criticize the actors.

As rehearsals progressed, I grew to admire Mr. Smith. He was a real professional, and he was talented. We both shared a common dream of using drama to minister. We spent a lot of time "talking shop" together. In fact, we started spending so much time working together that Dr. Dalan suspected that I was neglecting my other class work. She was right.

It was Mr. Smith who gave me the best compliment I had ever received. I was to meet him at his office one morning to do some work on the set for the play. I didn't find him in his office so I started walking down the hallways hoping he would see me. After about 20 minutes of searching, I heard his voice in front of me. He was talking to another student. I caught up with him and asked him if we were still going to work together that day.

"Didn't you see the note on my door?"

"What?"

"Oh Joe, I'm sorry! I forgot you were blind!"

He forgot I was blind! That was the nicest thing anyone had ever said to me! I laughed so hard that I nearly cried as we walked back to the drama department.

Through the weeks that followed I did everything I could to work on the play. I poured glue, painted canvas, hammered nails, hunted down props, and just plain got in the way. But I didn't care. As long as I was working on the set, I was no longer "blind" or "sighted"; I was simply Joe Ransom doing what Joe Ransom does best. And I loved it!

One day about a week before opening night, Mr. Smith called me into his office before rehearsal. "Joe, the programs are being made for the play. I've put your name in the program"

"Thank you."

"Do you know where I put your name?"

Did I hear a smile cross his face?

"Properties Man?"

"No. I gave you the title 'Assistant Director'."

Assistant Director! I was speechless. Mr. Smith was showing me that I had proven myself to him. I had gained his respect, and I will always be grateful to him for that.

One night as the cast was putting on their makeup and costumes for rehearsal, Mr. Smith asked me if I would do him a favor.

"Sure, I will."

"Will you please go to the store and pick up some color film for my camera? I want to take pictures of tonight's rehearsal."

"Of course."

I thought to myself for a minute and then said; "Sir, do you know what this looks like? A blind man buying color film for a camera?"

I could still hear him laughing with the cast as I closed the door at the end of the hallway.

The play was a brilliant success and we were all proud of Mr. Smith and his cast and crew. Only an actor can appreciate the pain we felt as we tore down the set. Every time I tear down the set of a play, I feel as if a part of me is being torn apart.

But life goes on.

After the play was over and the end of the school year approached, I began to think more seriously of my future. I still did not know exactly what God wanted me to do after graduation, and it made me uncomfortable. I spent a lot of time praying with Rick and Ric about God's will for our lives. I was seeing my need to be closer to God and my need to be conformed to His image. God had to be first place in my life, and I wasn't sure that He was.

After my final trailer payment had been made in February (exactly one year after my trailer fire), some students helped me move my trailer closer to campus. Now, instead of spending most of my day walking back and forth to school, I was able to spend most of my day studying and seeking answers from God concerning my future.

One morning shortly after my move closer to campus, I was called into the financial aid office.

"Sir, I was told you wanted to see me."

"Yes, Joe. We just received a phone call asking us if we knew of any students in a real financial need. Naturally, I thought of you. The caller, who wished to remain anonymous, wants to pay for all of your meals in the cafeteria for the rest of the school year!"

I still did not know where God wanted me in the future, but He was showing me that He was meeting my needs on a day-to-day basis. God knew the future; I need only concern myself with today.

Toward the end of the semester Evangel had a conference in which representatives from schools all across the United States interviewed prospective teachers for their schools.

The interviews were held in the school library. I had never had a reason to use the school library, so I was unfamiliar with the building. Joe Teeter led me to the upstairs section where the interviews would be held, and I walked around the small room until I had a clear picture of it in my mind. The next day I was ready for my first interview.

I walked into the room and with my back to the school representatives, I slipped my folded cane under the receptionist's desk. I walked slowly to the desk of my first interview and sat down prepared to answer his questions.

I fully intended to tell him I was blind, but I wanted to wait until the end of the interview. I wanted to at least have a chance for a normal interview.

About half-way through the interview the gentleman brought out pictures of his school to show me. That was my clue to tell him I was blind.

I never knew that silence could be so loud. He was quiet for about 30 seconds and then finished the interview as if nothing out of the ordinary had happened.

After the interview one of the secretaries that had witnessed the incident stopped me as I was leaving the room.

"Joe, I'm ashamed of you! That was totally uncalled for. You should have told him at the beginning that you were blind."

"But if I had, he probably would not have given me an interview. Believe me, I'm speaking from experience."

"Well, I don't believe you!"

"OK, I'll prove it! I have another interview in 10 minutes. You have my permission to eavesdrop on our conversation. I will tell him at the very beginning that I am blind. You can see for yourself that I am right."

I sat down for the interview as I had done for the previous interview. After we introduced ourselves and shook hands I said, "Sir, I think you should know from the start that I am blind. I don't consider it a handicap however and -"

"I'm sorry, I don't think it will be necessary for you to fill out an application. We're looking for another type of person."

To be fair, I must say that not all of the gentlemen treated me this way. Many of them were kind and gave me a fair chance, but because many of them acted as this man did, I found it necessary to play along until I felt it was the proper time for me to tell them about my blindness.

As graduation came closer and closer, I began to think more about my family. I had seen one of my brothers and two of my sisters the summer before, but I had not seen my father and step-mother in several years. I wanted so much for them to be proud of me. I wanted them to see me graduate, but I knew they could not make the trip from Montana.

I started to call them every week on the phone just to tell them how I was doing. It wasn't the same as being with them, but it was the next best thing. By now they knew that I was blind, and I wanted them to share my excitement at graduating from two colleges the same day.

Finally, the long-awaited day arrived. I traded my cowboy hat for a cardboard cap and my blue jeans for a black gown.

I was pleased and somewhat embarrassed when a reporter from the Springfield Leader & Press approached me for an interview as I waited to go into the auditorium.

As gracefully as I could, I walked down the aisle to my seat in the auditorium as I heard the processional march. I sat quietly as my thoughts tuned out the speaker, and my mind flowed freely to past days.

I remembered the day when I was 16 years old and my brother Randy said, "Joe, you'll never make it to college. You don't have enough common sense to make it on your own."

Like other graduates that day I had mixed emotions. I had finally done it. In one hour Ronald Joseph Ransom would be a college graduate! But I also had sad feelings that morning.

While other students whispered about their graduation gifts and plans to see their families, I felt sorry for myself.

I would have no graduation gifts. I did not have a family in the audience to cheer for me as I graduated. And I did not know where I would go after graduation.

Suddenly my thoughts were interrupted as we stood to walk the aisle and receive our diplomas. I could feel the blood rushing through my body as I walked toward the platform. No one else knew the victory that was mine alone.

Then it was my turn. As I heard my name being called and I reached for my degree and shook President Spence's hand, I barely heard him say, "We're very proud of you" over the roar of the crowd. As my name was called the entire auditorium filled with cheers and hand clapping, and I knew then that I was not alone. I was receiving the greatest graduation gift any man could ever have.

I also knew that I had been wrong. I had lived for this day for years. It was my only goal, and I had reached it. But I was wrong in seeing this day as the climax, for it was only the beginning. I did not attain that day; I merely left the womb. There would be new goals and new fights. There would be new failures and new victories.

No matter what the future brought; no matter where God would lead, Joe Ransom would never be alone again.

  *And now for the rest of the story… (well, almost)*

Then…   Not long ago…

It has been more than forty years since I graduated from Evangel College and Central Bible College. What in the world has happened since then?

For the past forty-plus years I have been active in a variety of ministries. After completing my graduate studies I spent several years managing personal care homes in Georgia and Tennessee. At the same time, I began traveling as an evangelist/dramatist. Eventually I returned to the Springfield, MO area where I taught in both private and public schools while beginning my new career as a playwright and stage director. After several years working as the Managing Director of Stained Glass Theatre, my wife, Kaye, and I moved to Mississippi to be nearer to family. My wife and I still continue my dream of 'trying to win my world to Jesus Christ through drama' with the ministry of 'Joseph's Closet,' where I travel portraying Bible characters. And I continue writing and directing stage plays while working on other writing and ministry projects. One of my next projects will be a more complete, closer to the end, almost all of it, pretty much up to date, nearly finished, not much left to the imagination sequel to *I'm Not Really Blind, I Just Can't See.*

Complete Works from Joseph Ransom

The Healing City-A Cowboy Christmas Story
(novel version)

I'm Not Really Blind, I Just Can't See
(Autobiography)

Building the Church Together *(Seven Weeks of Individual and Corporate Prayer)*

(Stage Plays)

Unto the Least of These   *(The story of George Mueller)*

Songs in the Night *(The story of Fanny Crosby)*

Woven in Time *(A Christmas story of love, war, and hope)*

Not Many Noble *(The story of D.L. Moody)*

The Christmas God Came to Dinner *(A true story of war and peace in WW11)*

Trumpets FromThe Rooftop *(The story of William and Catherine Booth)*

Compelled *(The story of William Carey)*

The Last Oasis *(The story of Lillian Trasher)*

I'm Not Really Blind, I Just Can't See *(Stage play by Ron Laws, adapted from the novel)*

The Healing City – A Cowboy Christmas Story *(stage version)*

Toys of War *(The Story of A.C. Gilbert)*

Amazing Grace *(The Story of John Newton and William Wilberforce)*

An Atheist in the Parsonage *(the story of Adoniram Judson)*

ABOUT THE AUTHOR

Dr. Ronald Joseph Ransom was born in Ronan, Montana. Upon graduation from college, he returned to the foothills of the Rockies for two months to write *I'm Not Really Blind, I Just Can't See* .

Upon completion of this book, Joseph (as he is now called) completed a Master's degree in Religious Education, a Doctorate of Ministries degree in Counseling, and a Doctorate of Theology degree, all from Antioch Seminary in Georgia.

Joseph is the founder of Joseph's Closet, a traveling drama ministry specializing in one-man Biblical presentations. He also travels as a motivational speaker, conference speaker and evangelist.

Joseph is the author of *The Healing City*, a novel based on his stage play by the same name. In addition, he has written numerous other stage plays.